500

CW01464330

DOWN BY THE HEAD

By

Captain G.H.Handbury-Grassick

DOWN BY THE HEAD

Cover design by
Ossie Jones Liverpool

Copyright G Handbury-Grassick
First published in 2003 by Lane Publishers

ISBN 1897666 39 9

£17.95

Artwork and Graphics By Lane Publishers

DOWN BY THE HEAD

By G Handbury-Grassick

A dedication to all those men who went down to the sea in ships many never to return

PROLOGUE

The War at Sea started with the sinking of the "ATHENIA" on September 3rd 1939.

The ship was carrying children being evacuated to Canada . The German U Boat was lying in wait for them. It ended 5yrs-8 months & 4 days later.

The last ship to be sunk was the Avondale Park on the 7th. May 1945.

Each May The Merchant Navy observe the last of the great celebrations of the end of the war in Europe. Hopefully it will go some way towards rekindling that sense of comradeship that bound our country together so effectively during those six dark years. A spirit that is remembered with pride by those who were part of it.

This year on the evening of May 8th, we all stood in silence to remember with sorrow and gratitude those who did not survive that bitter struggle which threatened to engulf the world.

The number of men who lost their lives on both sides at sea was greater than the combined deaths in all the naval battles of the previous 500 years.

5,150 Allied merchant ships were lost during the war. 2,828 of these were sunk by enemy submarines, mostly German U boats.

WE WILL REMEMBER THEM

UNTIL THE SEAS ARE NO MORE

Casualties were as follows
Merchant seamen

United Kingdom	22,490
Indian Lascars	6,093
Chinese	2,023
United States	5,662
Norway	4,795
Greece	2,000
Holland	1,914
Denmark	1,863
Canada	1,437
Belgium	893
South Africa	189
Australia	109
New Zealand	72

It is possible that as many as 6,500 merchant seamen from Neutral countries also died.

Gunners in Merchant ships who were killed

British	Royal Navy (D.E.M.S.)	2,713
Royal Maritime Regiment		1,222
American	U.S. Armed Guard	1,640 (to end of 1944 only)

U- BOAT LOSSES

Out of 1,131 U-boats commissioned, 785 were lost.

Out of 863 U-boats that actually sailed on operational patrols, 754 were sunk.

Of 39,00 men who went to sea in U-boats, the U-boat Memorial at Laboe, Kiel, records the names of 27,491 who died.

5,000 became prisoner of war.

Ratings who were taken prisoner were returned to their families after several months, but many U-boat officers were dismayed to find they were regarded as a special catagory of prisoner.

The Allies regarded them as the most fanatical of Nazis (many had been very truculent when captured — arrogant is the word frequently used by their captors) and that if they returned to a recently defeated Germany they might form the core of a Resistance groups — "Werewolf groups" was the vogue phrase of the period.

Many U boat officers were kept prisoner until well into 1947; when they were released they were more than grateful to settle down to a quiet life with little inclination to take to the woods. Instead they were a little surprised to find that they were soon being courted to serve in the re-born German Navy when Germany was invited to join N.A.T.O. A harsher fate fell on Admiral Donitz. He was put on trial with the German War Criminals at Nuremberg and charged on three counts. He was found guilty on two counts and sentenced to serve 10 years in prison. He served the full term being released in 1956. He died in 1980 aged 89.

INDEX

Page	Chapter	Details
Page	Chapter	
4		PROLOGUE
7		PREFACE
8		FOREWORD
14		ACKNOWLEDGEMENTS
15	ONE	MY EARLY YEARS
20	TWO	HMS GANGES/HMS WELLESLEY
29	THREE	S.S BOTAVON
40	FOUR	CONVOY PQ 15
48	FIVE	S.S BOTAVON TO MV PARDO
94	SIX	D.E.M.S BARRACKS BOMBAY/ S.S YOMA
103	SEVEN	M V NEDERLAND
112	EIGHT	M V GASCONY
152	NINE	ON LEAVE THEN BACK TO D.E.M.S LIVERPOOL
156	TEN	M V EMPIRE FLINT
168	ELEVEN	EMPIRE FLINT TO HOME
175	TWELVE	M V ORESTES
190	THIRTEEN	M V FORT McDONNELL
195	FOURTEEN	M V CILICIA
199	FIFTEEN	M V STAFFORDSHIRE
202	SIXTEEN	M V EMPRESS OF SCOTLAND

PREFACE

My interest in the sea was aroused many years ago when I was a boy. I was an avid reader of the "Wizard", a Boy's magazine costing 2 pence. One particular week there was an article about Sir Stanford Raffles, the Founder of Singapore, and the front page showed a photograph of a Blue Funnel ship arriving in port. From that moment on my ambition was to one day see for myself this foreign land. This I achieved at the age of 25 when I signed on my first Blue Funnel ship, a 27 year old coal-burning ship, the S.S. "Atreus".

I stayed at sea until July 1969 and witnessed the gradual demise of our once great fleet of Merchant ships. First came the super tankers that were first introduced by a Greek ship owner, followed by bulk carriers of which I used to give a wide berth. Finally, the great huge container ships, the introduction of which brought about the closure of huge dock areas and cargo sheds, while not forgetting the disappearance of thousands of our Merchant Navy seamen and dock workers.

FOREWORD

by
R Purvis

This is the story of the Battle of the Atlantic and Far East stations from the eyes of a Royal Naval Gunner who served in Merchant vessels as a D.E.M.S. Gunner (Defensively Equipped Merchant Ships) in that theatre of war.

I have personally known the author for some forty three years, and having been shipmates together (though not in war time), have experienced similar weather conditions as he experienced on convoy duties during the winter in the North Atlantic; in the area Halifax, Nova Scotia, plus Saint Johns New Brunswick, Saint Johns Newfoundland and Mid Atlantic with force ten gales, snow, ice, fog and rain; experienced the rolling of vessels to the extent of losing the bridge wing as they dipped. Also, the incident of dumping locomotives which had broken loose from their chained fastenings. Due to the severe weather conditions in the Atlantic, such things also happened to convoys bound for the United Kingdom with urgently needed supplies, such as tanks, landing craft and aircraft.

The following story commences in the tiny village of New Tupton in Derbyshire, just recently bombed by the Luftwaffe returning from a bombing raid of the munition factories of Sheffield. The pilots had to get rid of their bombs and decided to drop them on an innocent English village, killing many civilians, one being the cousin of the author and her three children. The author tried to join the Royal Navy at the age of seventeen and a half, but was told to come back when he was eighteen! The day he became eighteen he once again went to Derby for his medical examination and was accepted the very same day, the year was 1940. He was immediately drafted to H.M.S. Ganges for basic seamanship training, and after completing his three months, he was drafted to H.M.S. Wellesley for gunnery training relevant to "Tribal Class" destroyers and their type of armament. Alas, after training finished there, he was posted to Leith to join an ancient Merchant Vessel, the S.S. Botavon, saved from the scrap yard under the British Government's policy to refurbish old vessels which were still serviceable but uninsurable due to age. The Board of Trade took out the insurance and the ships were managed by private companies. Some thirty-six vessels were re-commissioned at a time when the "Wolf" packs of U-boats were reaping havoc

8

to the British and allied Merchant fleets in the Atlantic.

The S.S. Botavon proceeded in convoy from Leith to the Gulf of Mexico, then up the Mississippi to Port Sulphur to load sulphur for the British war effort, returning via the Gulf of Mexico again where the crew experienced the joys of prickly heat rash due to their inexperience of the tropical climate, and battle clothing issues unsuited for such weather conditions.

The United States provided escort vessels to the convoy assembly point between the United States and Halifax, thence British and Canadian escorts across the U-boat infested Atlantic to Liverpool to discharge the sulphur cargo.

On arrival at Liverpool, all the D.E.M.S. Gunners were transferred to other vessels requiring gunners to take them to awaiting convoys bound for various ports around the world as trade demanded.

The title of this book came from a vessel the author served on during his service as a D.E.M.S. Gunner, which crossed the South Atlantic under atrocious conditions of fog, ice and gales, with her cargo of manganese ore so vital to the war effort. It describes the hardships encountered on the voyage, water rationing and very little food until they came across one of the lifeboats of S.S. Orcades – minus any survivors, but fully stored. It was lifted aboard and the crew's rations were replenished from the contents of its food lockers.

The recovery of this lifeboat took place off the island of Tristan Da Cunha – the whole area was being patrolled by U-boats and German raiders.

The author gives accounts of the ten vessels he served on during his time as a D.E.M.S. Gunner. Also, the shock at seeing and taking on board survivors from the Japanese prisoner of war camps as they began their journey back to the United Kingdom for treatment for their horrific wounds, starvation and the appalling conditions they experienced during their captivity.

R. Purvis

The gun crew closed up at their gun a Four inch, dual purpose both surface and Ack-Ack using fixed ammunition. A damn sight quicker than the old World War one monstrosities (Shell, cordite & percussion tube.)

The Deadliest of close range weapons, is how experienced D.E.M.S. Gunners describe the Oerlikon 20mm., gun shown here

On the way to Benghazi. The gun crew of a merchantman doing a practice shoot with their 12 pounder Anti-Aircraft gun. The Boatswain (right) passes the ammunition.

D.E.M.S. Gunners of the Maritime Royal Artillery manning a Bofors 40mm., gun

Watching the sky for enemy aircraft. Soldiers of the maritime Ack-Ack, with the famous Lewis 3.03

65 years old A.B.Moy Jones manning the Hotchkiss Machine Gun on board the "Melita". A reliable gun but you had to hold your fire for them to be effective. I shot down a Jap Dive Bomber. "A Zero" We did not have the Oerikon 20mm., in those days.

A group of our British merchant seamen receiving instruction from a Gunnery C.P.O.

A French Browning machine gun in action. A very capable gun. When I was on the M.V. Gascony two American gunners came aboard with them (The armed Guard) from Bahia all the way to Trinidad.

ACKNOWLEDGEMENTS

Harry Milsom, Editor of "Sea Breezes", who assisted me with my early research.
Ruth Barriskill, Corporation of London Libraries.
David Ashby, Naval Historical Branch, Ministry of Defence, Lloyds Register.
P. Francine Holdgate, Photograph Archives, Imperial War Museum.
Public Record Office, Kew.
Mrs. M. Sampson, Curator, National Maritime Museum.
Margaret Evans, Archives, National Museum & Galleries, Liverpool.
Captain Simpson, The Merchant Navy Association.
Ronald Purvis, Merchant Navy, Retired. Now living in Australia.
Sgt. Ray Hubbard and Dr. Kenneth Trigg for Japanese P.O.W. photographs.
Jim Passey, Ex. 4th Regiment Maritime Royal Artillery, for D.E.M.S. and Maritime strengths and casualties.
Lionel Wheble.
Ronald G. Gardner, D.E.M.S. Gunner.
Mrs. D.M. Bryan, "Blue Funnel" Liverpool.
Cliff Parsons, World Ship Society.
Captain Hall, Ship Search, Marine, Canada.
Mr. Todd, National Maritime Museum.
Alison Duffield and John Delaney, Imperial War Museum.
E.M. Sewells, Liverpool.
Alison Handley, Public Service Enquiries, R/N Gosport.
Iain Mackensie, Maritime Information Centre.
David Sibley (Retired) Merchant Navy Officer.
Peter Kemp, Imperial War Museum.
David Hughes, Durban.
Carl Newton, Cape Town.
Jurgen Rohwer, Author of "Axis Submarine Attacks World War Two".
Thomas Weis, The "U" Boat Photo Laboratory, Stuttgart.
U.S. Navy Archives, Washington, D.C.
David Bell, Imperial War Museum.

CHAPTER I

MY EARLY YEARS

I was born on my grandmother's farm at 05.30 hours on June 17th 1922 and brought into the world by my grandmother who had been a midwife. I had a sister Kathleen, and a brother, John. There was two years difference between our ages. I was the youngest. Mother did not enjoy good health and had periodic spells in Sheffield Infirmary. She was one of nine children, having four brothers and four sisters.

Father was the breadwinner, working for grandfather Handbury, driving his huge Burrell traction engine to pull the threshing equipment and haul out the huge trees that his sons (Arthur, Harry, John and Fred) felled. This was done the hard way, sharp axe and large crosscut saw. In areas that were inaccessible for his teams of giant Shire horses they had to manually haul the trees out and load them onto the 'Drugs'. It was a means of a steady income for grandfather to clothe and feed his big family. He was in charge of the felling and hauling of the trees that were eventually taken to his brother Tom's saw mill.

With mother being ill, I was brought up on the home farm. At that time grandfather owned three. Mother died when I was three years old. Brother John and myself went to live with grandmother Handbury. My father and sister, Kathleen, vacated our farm cottage and went to live with grandmother Grassick.

When I was four years old, I started school and this involved a walk of a mile and a half, there being no transport. I had my lunch with an Aunt and her twins, Dorothy and Arthur. Before I was five, grandmother's two youngest daughters, Alice and Dolly, were married and had a double wedding. I was then taken to live with my Aunt Alice and her husband Lloyd who went to live on one of grandfather's farms, and to get them started in life he would only charge a peppercorn rent. This farm was about two and a half miles from school and I used to meet up with the local blacksmith's daughter Dorothy, at the top of the lane. Only on very wet days were we taken to school in style.

My uncle had a very old car – a CLYNO –, which had a dickey seat, so we really enjoyed our ride to school on wet days. I well remember these walks to school, both of us children carrying a small medicine bottle filled with milk, and a sandwich and apple.

Our teacher was my cousin Sally. She was a big woman and took a sadistic delight in using a twelve-inch ruler to cane us across our bare knuckles if anyone dare disobey her.

When I was about five years old, my aunt and uncle had to move off the farm as another of grandfather's sons got married and he, in his turn, had the farm at a peppercorn rent. Aunt Alice and her husband bought a new farm about four miles away. We were situated right on the edge of a mining village called New Tupton. All the miners worked at one of three colleries – Clay Cross, Grassmoor or Pilsley. I remember the long rows of small miner's homes, with no bathroom and an outside toilet. But it was a way of life that has thankfully gone now. New Tupton was a little compact village, with two public houses, a Miners Welfare Club, a Co-operative; two fish and chip shops, newsagents and a greengrocer. There was also a fairly large council school. You stayed here until the age of fourteen, which was the school leaving age at the time. This was my third school but I quickly found new friends. On reflection, the standard of schooling was fairly good. We had sports and swimming and I obtained third, second and first swimming certificates, and also my Life Saving Certificate. Little did I realize this was to be an asset in later years when I ran away to sea. I practiced very hard at soccer and used to run round the fields at the farm to give me staying power. I wanted to get into the school soccer team, for this meant a Saturday morning off from the farm work! Farm work was hard and everyone worked, including me. My jobs were mucking out the cows and pigsties and chicken sheds, and chopping up giant heaps of straw and crushing swedes to mix with linseed cake for the cows to be fed twice a day. There were 16 cows on the farm, all milked by hand. I also had various jobs to do before I left for school in the morning, i.e. get the fire started in the kitchen, feed the two pigs and hens. My next job was to fill the drinking trough for the horses and cows. This was the toughest job I had to do for it involved pumping the water up by hand from an underground well – we had no automatic drinking bowls. Believe me, I did enjoy my breakfast after this hard task! Unfortunately, I would get so tired that I would fall asleep over my lessons at school, to be woken up by a prod with a cane by whoever was teaching us!

I enjoyed school and looked forward to the history, geometry and woodwork classes. I also learned to play the pipes and was in the school pipe band. After the 1928 recession, things got extremely tough on the farms, as it did everywhere else. Although I was very young at the time, I have vivid memories of the "Jarrow Hunger Marchers" marching through Chesterfield. It was on a Saturday morning. I used to help my uncle with the milk round at week-ends and we had just come out of a small street on the main Chesterfield to Derby road. (This was the same route as Bonnie Prince Charlie had trodden in 1746 on his way to London.) We pulled up to let them pass. They all looked gaunt and hungry and many had their feet wrapped with strips of cloth and tied with string. My uncle said they didn't have any food and put some money in their collecting buckets. I can remember feeling very sorry for these men and adding my sixpence piece to the collection. They were a very brave body of workers and this episode has always stayed in my mind.

My aunt and uncle were having difficulty keeping the farm going and their mort-gage commitments. Many farmers went bankrupt. At the time it was suggested that if the farm were sold I would go and live with my aunt's sister. However, somehow the money was raised and I stayed on at the farm.

I left school before my fourteenth birthday and I never remember anyone ask-ing why I wasn't attending school. I now worked on the farm full time taking the place of one of the labourers who was dismissed. I was paid one shilling a week! We all worked from 6 a.m. to 7 or 8 p.m. in the winter. In the summer when we were harvesting we were out in the fields until 10 p.m. or even later. I was also learning to plough with the horses and I was fond of them all. There was Old Blossom, Dyna and Dick, the Shire horses, and then Stanley, an old pit pony who we adopted. He was really loveable and would pull the milk float around Chesterfield.

The milk from the farm had to be taken to Clay Cross station to get the 7 a.m.

Milk train to Sheffield as we supplied a retailer there. I was also given a milk round in the village. I started with just five gallons a day in 1936 but it wasn't long before it built up to 15 gallons. Milk was not delivered in bottles at this time. It was carried in churns and one would carefully measure each pint and this would be poured into a jug which the housewife would hand you.

Entertainment was a visit to the cinema on a Saturday night and maybe Sunday afternoons cycling with friends around the lanes and village. We rarely saw a car on our excursions.

Everyone of my generation will remember where they were on September 3rd 1939. I was delivering milk on this Sunday and was invited in by a neighbour to listen to Neville Chamberlain's speech. On the Monday, I took the horse and cart to get timber to make blackout shutters – and these had to be fitted every night and taken down in the morning.

From the time war was declared a complete change came over the village. Strict blackout precautions were enforced, and car headlamps were masked so that just a small light shone – sufficient to see directly in front of you. The local branch of the ARP was duly formed. There was a station and the ARP underwent regular practice drills. Conscription quickly followed and some of my older schoolmates were called up. My brother was the first conscript to be called up in Derbyshire, and I remember this fact being recorded in the Derbyshire Times. I'm happy to say he survived the war and was Mentioned in Dispatches during the Italian campaign. My sister joined the A.T.S. and I hardly saw them at all during the war years.

In January 1940 I went to Derby to enlist in the Royal Navy. I was not then 18. My Aunt informed the Recruiting Officer and I was told I would have to wait until my eighteen birthday. So it was back to the farm!

In early 1940 most of our major cities had been the targets for heavy bombing raids. There was a devastating raid on Sheffield and one of the enemy planes on the way back to Germany dropped a stick of three bombs over our small village of New Tupton. Every one scored a direct hit on three houses. Thirteen people were killed in a matter of seconds and, of course, I knew them all. Some of my schoolmates who I remember well had already been killed on active service and I was impatient to join the Forces.

On June 17th 1940 I again enlisted for the Royal Navy. I remember receiving a very piercing glare from the Recruiting Officer when I asked him to move my name to the top of the page as I had tried to enlist six months earlier. His remarks were "Go home and wait lad"; "I will do what I can"!

The type of Smoke Float we used to carry on the stern of Merchant ships. They were used by some fast Merchant ships to make good an escape. They were no good for the old tramp ships that had to struggle to work up a speed of 8 knots to keep up with the convoy.

Chapter 2

H.M.S. GANGES and H.M.S. WELLESLEY

I received my call up papers on January 21st 1941, instructing me to report to H.M.S. Ganges, near Ipswich, on February 3rd.   This was a Monday – I remember as some of my Aunt's friends insisted on giving me a small farewell party. One of the ladies gave me a Saint Christopher and instructed me to wear it at all times and I would survive the war. I bought a cheap chain and wore it until I swallowed the anchor late 1969. I left Chesterfield that day and on arrival at Ipswich, we were met by R.N. Transport and taken to H.M.S. Ganges at Shotly. We were soon allocated to a hut. Mine was at the bottom of the long covered way, which we soon discovered was an extremely long way from the parade ground! The huts were fitted with two-tier bunks. I managed to get a top one, our mattress being the one taken out of our hammock. We also had a very thick white blanket. The top end of the hut was our "mess deck" with one long table at each side which was also used for recreation. After a quick meal we had a medical check and an inoculation.

Getting kitted out did not take long. Hold open your kit bag and the various items of seaman's kit was thrown in. My trousers were about a foot too long but the tailor's shop appeared to work overtime to get us all ready for parade the next day. The daily roster was quickly sorted out by two efficient Chief Petty Officers, CPO Eccles and CPO Fairbrother. Between them they taught us parade ground drill, seamanship and gunnery. Both of our CPO's had served all their years in the Royal Navy. When it was your turn to be "Peggy" (to get the food from the galley), one had to get a move on as we were some distance from the galley. The food was of a high standard, and later in the evening we were provided with cocoa. This ensured a good night's sleep.

For anyone who was not too particular with their personal cleanliness there were compulsory showers under the watchful eye of the P.T. Instructor. Everyone had to pass the Royal Navy swimming test. To do this you had to wear a white "duck suit", dive in at the deep end and swim one length of the baths. The other test was to climb the rigging of the mast at the side of the parade ground. This did not present a problem to some of us as we had been practising at the end of the day. They told us that if you went up and over the "futtocks" instead of the easy way through the "lubbers hole" you were given higher marks. I managed to get a 72 hour pass before completing my training. It was a long train journey from Ipswich to Derbyshire but it was nice to get home and enjoy some home cooking. Everyone commented that I had lost weight. It was soon time to return but there was an air raid during the journey and my train was delayed for two hours. It did not occur to me to get some sort of proof from the Station Master or the Military Police. I arrived back at H.M.S. Ganges two hours late and was immediately put on charge and told to appear before the Captain the following day. I was marched in left right, left right, halt, off cap, don't move. The charge was read out. All I could say was that I had not been told to get proof of any delay during travel. "No excuse" said the Captain. "I award you two hours work in the galley after gunnery classes for four days". So I had to report after the evening meal to the Duty Cook, along with a few more defaulters. The punishment was peeling potatoes! About half a ton. The Cook allowed us to smoke and gave us as much tea as we wanted and also a sandwich, so all in all it wasn't too bad a punishment.

When our Course was over I was drafted to H.M.S. Pembroke (Chatham) and arrived there on 11th April 1941. The barracks were much the same but we did have a separate Mess Deck. Before dusk we took our hammocks into a huge tunnel which acted as our shelter in the event of air raids. We were all waiting for a posting and it was rumoured that we were going to be part of the crew of a new Tribal Class Destroyer that was being commissioned at Chatham. We were then told to report to the Drill Shed for an address by the Captain. He gave us an up-to-date account of the war at sea and the sorry plight of our Merchant Navy, whose losses were horrendous. They were being decimated hourly by German U-boats. Defence systems were being put aboard as quickly as possible and most of us would be drafted to Liverpool to the DEMS (Defensively Equipped Merchant Ships). We arrived at H.M.S. Wellesley on 26th April 1941 and very quickly got allocated to what was going to be our home for the next three weeks. Once again we got muscled into more gunnery and again had efficient Instructors. They taught us how to handle the 6-inch and 4-inch surface guns and the 12 pounder. Also the Lewis, Marlin and Hotchkis machine guns for use against aircraft. Not forgetting the Holman Projector and FAMS (Fast Aerial Mines). Also the use of smoke-floats and depth charges. The 40-mm Bofors and the 20-mm Oerlikon were not included during our Course.

It was while we were having our training that the German High Command made Liverpool their target. We had been having some warm weather and very moonlight nights and all the German bomber pilots had to do was to follow the River Mersey to the docks and release their loads of death and destruction. They were always led by bombers which carried incendiaries to light up the target area. We would take it in turns to do fire-watching on the Hospital roof, as this Barracks had been the old Southern General Hospital. One night we received a direct hit. The only casualties were some of the gunners returning from a few hours ashore. Our shelters were underneath the Hospital, the storerooms and morgue. There were about 20 people in our shelter and when the bomb struck we were covered with plaster and debris, the entrance door was also jammed with bricks and falling masonry. One of the seamen next to me became hysterical so I had to slap him across the face and tell him to calm down, which he did. The following day apologised for his behaviour. When they dug us out I had a good long look at the bombed area. It reminded me of what I saw when my village was bombed and I had to gaze on the rubble of what was once my cousin's house and where she and her two daughters were killed. The Ladies W.V.S. van quickly arrived on the site and they gave us all mugs of tea, biscuits and cake – and also cigarettes.

On 17th May our gunnery Course was completed and we were awarded our Seaman's Gunners Badge and, if I remember correctly, an increase of three-pence per day! I was now getting about nineteen shillings and sixpence per week as a Seaman Gunner – more than I was earning before I enlisted. We were all sent on a few days leave, taking our kit with us. This now

22

consisted of two large kit bags and our hammock. We were told to always carry a civilian suit when overseas in case our ship called at a neutral country. If we went ashore wearing our Naval uniforms we could be arrested as spies.

It was while I was on embarkation leave that H.M.S. Hood was sunk by the German Battleship "Bismark" on 24th May 1941. There were only three survivors. I received a telegram from DEMS Liverpool to report immediately to DEMS Leith. I arrived there on May 25th.

The U.S.S. Washington and H.M.S. Duke of York. Escorts for Convoy P.Q.15 Reykavic to Murmansk. Sailed 26.04.1942 arrivd 6.05.1942

The huge hole in the bows of H.M.S. King George V as she readies for her return to U.K. for repairs after a collision with H.M.S. Punjabi, "Tribal class destroyer" escorting convoy P.Q.15, there were only 208 survivors

The U.S.S. Tuscaloosa one of the escorts for convoy P.Q.15. Reykjavic to Murmansk sailed 26.04.1942 arrived 06.05.1942

Captain F.J.Walker's ship H.M.S. Starling. Depth charge party at the traps prepare for action.

Heinkel He 111 aircraft in formation. They operated from bases in "Norway" to attack the Russian convoys. They sank the "S.S. Botavon" Convoy P.Q.15 her gunners shot down two enemy aircraft, who had assisted in the sinking of H.M.S. "Trinidad"

H.M.S. Punjabi "Tribal class destroyer", sunk by H.M.S. King George V while engaged in escorting convoy P.Q.15 to Russia. Murmansk, Russia. Sadly only 208 survived this most horrendous collision.

The pilot of the Hawker Sea Hurricane receiving final instructions before climbing into his plane on the catapult. Very brave pilots. Out of reach of land they had to ditch into the sea and rely on being picked up. "We salute them all".

H.M.S.Trinidad taken from H.M.S.Fury in a North Atlantic snow storm. She went to Murmansk and picked up 40 survivors from Botavon but unfortunately she was sunk on May 14th. by Heinkell 111 Torpedo Bombers

SS-Botavon, Gross tons 5848 Built by Chas O'Connell Glasgow 1912 as INDRAKUALA for Thos B-Royden& Co Acquired when Royden fleet joined the Ocean SS-Co and was renamed Eurppylus. In 1938. sold to Continental Transit Co and renamed Trade. Purchased by the Board of Trade in 1939 and renamed BOTAVON (My First ship) Sadly she was sunk on the 3rd may 1943

Chapter 3

SS "BOTAVON"

The only duty one had to carry out while in barracks at Leith was A.R.P. A party of us had a trip out to the gunnery range to do a practice shoot with the 12 Pounder Ack-Ack and the small arms 303 machine-guns. When on shore leave a group of us would sometimes take the long walk up to Princes Street. We quickly discovered that the Scottish beer was very palatable and the Scots hospitable.

Time seemed to drag until I was drafted to my first ship, a weather beaten coal-burning tramp the ss "Botavon". The first time I saw her, the dockers were discharging her cargo of scrap metal which she had brought over from America. It was being discharged by huge magnets, one to each hold, and dumped into railway trucks on the wharf. I was directed to the gunners' accommodation and was met by the Gunlayer in charge of both Navy and Army gunners. I was allocated a lower bunk, which proved to be a blessing because later on when we ran into bad weather I suffered from seasickness. After a mug of tea and a cigarette, the Gunlayer, Jack Sparry, said he would take me along to the Ship's saloon and get me signed on the Ships Articles. Someone from the Shipping Office was there signing on crew members. I met the Ship's Master, Captain Isaacs, who remarked "We are your first ship, keep a sharp look out, and good luck". Then he was gone.

Signing on was new to me, as I had never set foot on a ship before. The Shipping Master duly entered my name, home address and next of kin in the Ships Articles, also my scale of wages which was a set rate for all DEMS gunners of sixpence per day, three shillings and sixpence per week. The next thing was to be introduced to the rest of the gunners, Ted Lewis, who was from Liverpool and proved to be a very good mate, and Bill Lovatt who came from the south of England. The remaining two were army gunners, part of the Maritime Ack-Ack. They came aboard with

29

their own Lewis machine guns which fired a 303 bullet and were loaded into round pans which held fifty rounds. Their names were Bob "call me Paddy" Hutson, whose deep Irish brogue and good sense of humour would quickly dispel any form of discontent, and Harry Crabtree, who was a quiet man who came from London and liked nothing better than to read. A roster was kept on the notice board and we took turns to clean our accommodation and scrub the mess room table. We slept and ate in the same space and we had a Bogey (a coal-burning stove) in the middle of the room. We also took turns to be "Peggy" (which meant getting the food from the galley).

After dinner we went up onto the gun deck and uncovered the 4 inch B.L. gun and the 12 Pounder and gave them both a thorough clean and oil and put the heavy canvas covers back on. We were later informed that we would be having gun drill the following day, along with members of the crew. The cargo of scrap metal was still being discharged and the Bosun told me that it would take another ten days to finish the work. Ted Lewis gave me a tour of the ship, starting off on the fo'c's'le head, up onto the boat deck, and then into the chartroom where the Second Mate was busy with his chart corrections. At the time they made little sense to me. Years later I was doing the very same thing, and cursing a Second Mate who had not kept the charts up to date! From the bridge we went aft and up onto the poop deck where our 4 inch gun was mounted. Everything was falling into place and I began to feel at home. We called in at the galley and I met Wally the cook, who explained the workings of the coal-burning galley stove. He warned us not to let the stove go out while he was on watch below, as it would mean a late breakfast!

We eventually got back to our accommodation in time for our evening meal. I went along with one of the lads to the galley and was shown the quickest way to get our food back to the mess deck before it got cold. After our meal I settled down, sent a letter home giving them the name of my first ship and address for mail, opened up my kit bag and got my gear stowed away in my locker. I finally clambered into my bunk about midnight. I could hear the drone of the generator but slept heavily. I was woken by Jack's alarm clock. "Your turn to make the tea, George" someone yelled out. Boiling water was supplied from a large copper tank that was connected to a steam pipe from the Engine Room and fitted with a brass tap.

After breakfast the Gunlayer told us we would be having a practice gun drill at 09.30 hrs. Our Gunnery Officer was the Second Mate, Mister Derry. The remaining members of the gun crew were made up of members of the crew who had attended gunnery classes at one of the DEMS Training Centres. They were the Bosun, Joe Blurton, A/B Ted Kimber, Arthur Day and the Second Steward, Percy Saville. The Second Mate satisfied himself that we all knew what we were supposed to know and then dismissed us. The dockers were still busy unloading and working late hours.

Four of us went ashore in the evening and took the tram all the way up Leith Walk to Princes Street. We called into a pub but had to make our drinks last as none of us had very much money. During the course of the evening we met a friendly Scot who insisted that we go home with him and meet his wife and teenage daughter. We had supper with them and it made a nice ending to our night out. The day before we sailed they invited us out again. In civilian life Jack worked for Cadburys, and they were very good in sending him (and other of their employees now in the armed forces) chocolate parcels. As he had recently received a parcel, he gave some of these to our new friend's wee daughter.

The dockers had all the cargo out by mid-day on the 16th June. The sailors got busy preparing the ship for sea and I watched with great interest. By this time I was getting more involved and somehow felt deep down that if I survived the war I would be staying in the Merchant Navy and making the sea my career. It was interesting to see the way the sailors dropped all the derricks into the crutches, put clamps on them and rope lashings; then on went the tarpaulins held down by locking bars, and at the sides and ends with wooden wedges. We sailed the following day – which was my nineteenth birthday and my first trip to sea. Soon after we dropped the Pilot we had boat drill. The Gunlayer set the watches and I was put on the 4 to 8 watch. Our course was round to Peterhead, Frazerburgh, Lossiemouth, and into the Moray Firth. Then through the Caledonian Canal to Oban, which was our convoy rendezvous. The weather was warm and sunny. Two of the sailors slung a pilot ladder over the side and those of us who felt tough enough dived overboard for a swim. No one stayed in for long as the water was cold. The Master was collected by Navy launch to get his sailing orders. We sailed the following day and joined up with convoy OB 339 which consisted of a total of 49 ships. We were the fourth ship of the first column. As we got away from the coast and further out to sea, we started to roll and pitch as we were in ballast. The weather gradually deteriorated and I quickly realised that my stomach was not as it should be. My four-hour watch on the gun deck seemed an eternity and whatever watch I happened to be on, I ate my meal quickly and then straight into my bunk. I was the only one out of all the gunners who got seasick, so I was the object of a lot of banter from them. The weather was deteriorating still further, grey skies and overcast and drizzle. The sea got rougher, making it difficult to stand. I did my watch and the only consolation from the rest of the gunners was "It will wear off after a few days". I became so seasick that the only thing I could keep down was toast or maybe some ship's biscuits.

Everyone in the ship knew I had not found my sea legs. The Master would ask Jack, or any of the lads who went on to the wings of the bridge, how I was going on and then it would be the usual reply "He'll be all right in a few days".

We had a good escort of both destroyers and corvettes. HMS Broadwater, HMS Burwell, HMS Leith, HMS Bittersweet and HMS Fennel.

The Commodore was Rear Admiral A.T. Tillard, DSO, RNR, in the Blue Funnel Cargo Passenger Ship "Myrmidon". This ship suffered many battle scars before she was finally sunk. In 1941, while lying at Hendersons Wharf, Birkenhead, during an air raid on May 13th 1941, a bomb exploded on the quay nearby. The ship was hauled off, but while crossing the dock she detonated an acoustic mine. The resulting damage caused her to settle on the bottom. After being raised and repaired she sailed on June 5th, only to set off a magnetic mine in the River Mersey. Following further repairs, she sailed again and was machine-gunned by aircraft off the Butt of Lewis in December. This time without suffering serious damage as no bombs were dropped. A few days later, she collided with a Norwegian ship which had just been launched at Clyde Bank, and both ships suffered damage. She was sunk on September 5th 1942 at 02.33 hours by the German U-boat U506, commanded by Commander Wurdemann. Position by German grid F.F. 2938. Our position states 00 degrees 45 minutes north. 06 degrees 27 minutes west. German Intelligence say convoy unknown, but the position was in the Gulf of Guinea. All 116 crew and 129 passengers were picked up by HMS Brilliant within a matter of hours. On July 1st 1941, at 09.40 hours, position 61 degrees 12 minutes north, 17 degrees 38 minutes west, HMS Bittersweet obtained a contact and carried out a depth charge attack and reported an oily patch. HMS Bittersweet subsequently lost contact and rejoined the convoy later. Unfortunately, it was learned later that HMS Burwell had been pumping out her bilges at the same time, hence the oil slick. Visibility became poor so the Bosun and two of the sailors had to stream the fog bouy. This was a clever devise. It was a strong piece of timber with a shackle at one end for the wire towing cable. The end that was in the water had a very strong galvanised bracket which scooped up the sea water and it sent up a flume of water 2' – 3' in height that the ship astern could see.

The convoy station keeping advised by the Admiralty was "500 metres for and aft and 1000 on the beam" or roughly about two and a half cables by five cables. We had further reinforcements mid ocean passage. HMS Richmond, HMS Ramsay, HMS Pollyanthus, HMS Cobalt and HMS Wolfe.

On July 8th at 23.50 hours, icebergs were sighted on the port side of the convoy. Then on July 10th at 04.00 hours the Commodore signalled that he thought it inadvisable to attempt a large alteration of course in such a dense fog. It was suggested that engines be stopped and ships dispersed to destinations in groups. At 04.27 hours the convoy stopped engines and hove to and turning together to starboard.

After the convoy was dispersed we proceeded on our own, and course was set for the Florida Straits, then into the Gulf of Mexico, the Mississippi River Delta, up the Mississippi to Port Sulphur. The weather got very hot and I suffered with what quite a lot of seafarers get in the tropics "prickly heat"! The only relief I found was during a tropical rainstorm, when I would strip off and stand out on deck! When we got alongside at Port Sulphur, which was just a long jetty, we discovered to our disappointment that we could not get ashore. Sulphur dust quickly covered the whole of the ship. Every door was kept closed but the fine yellow dust worked its way through the framework. Mosquitoes were another source of annoyance, but fortunately they did not attack me. When the dockers had finished at the end of the day, we would suspend pieces of oily rag soaked in paraffin under the door-frames and in the port holes and this helped to keep the mosquitoes at bay.

A large load of ships' stores arrived on the wharf and the Chief Steward asked the Bosun for some of the sailors to help get them aboard and along to the Store-room. One whole box of tomatoes disappeared into thin air and quite a few tins of food, so there was a lot of bad language from the Chief Steward! All the gunners had a clean slate as none of us had been asked to help. Later on a cardboard box containing a dozen large tomatoes and two tins of bully beef was left inside the entrance to our accommodation. We got a loaf of bread from the Cook and made beef and tomato sandwiches for a late snack!

We finally cast off and said farewell to Port Sulphur. The Bosun and the sailors got to work and flattened out the derricks, the tarpaulins spread, tucked in and wedged up and locking bars on again. The biggest job for them was washing down the ship. The sulphur had permeated everywhere. The day after sailing all the gunners got to work and gave the 4" B.L. and the 12 pounder a very thorough clean and oil. The Maritime gunners did likewise with their two Lewis guns, and the guns on the wings of the Bridge.

Jack, the Gunlayer, got some grey paint from the Bosun. He was a funny character and was never without his large Sherlock Holmes pipe and his headgear was a fighter Pilot's helmet which never came off his head no matter what the weather. I received some excellent seamanship tuition from one of the A.B.'s, Ted Kimba, who like all the rest of the A.B.'s had been at sea before the war. He taught me again the various knots and splices that I had been taught at HMS Ganges. He was also a good story-teller and his stories about Yokohama and the Dutch East Indies and Singapore were a never ending source of interest to me. Without a doubt he planted the seeds of wanderlust in me.

During the passage to Halifax, trouble arose in the Engine Room. One of the Lascar firemen attacked the engineer with a shovel and cut his back severely. The engineer had to be helped out and his wounds stitched. We heard afterwards that the engineer in question had been bullying this particular fireman, but what happened to him we did not find out. He was probably logged 10/- and given a bad report when he signed off.

We arrived in Halifax for our East bound convoy rendezvous. The Chief Steward sent word along that we could order certain rationed foods from the Chip's Chandler through him. We took advantage of this offer and were able to take home butter, sugar, tinned ham and tea, in quantities of 5 lbs.

No one was allowed ashore again but our stay at anchor was short-lived. Captain Isaacs was collected by Navy launch and went and received his sailing orders. This turned out to be the following day, August 1st 1941. During the early hours of August 1st 1941, we upped anchor and steamed out to join Convoy HX 142. When we got organised we were the eighth ship of the first column. Convoy total was 65 ships. The Commodore was Vice Admiral Sommerville, R.N.R. I discovered later that this was his 21st Convoy of the war. His ship was the "Manchester Exporter", the sixth ship of the first column. The Vice Commodore was Commodore Birnie, R.N.R. in the "Lock-Ewe", the first ship of the first column. The speed of the Convoy was regulated to 7 knots. We had one rescue ship, the "Perthshire", and two C.A.M. ships.

I did not know at the time that I was to sail in another Convoy with Commodore Birnie. This was Convoy S.C. 121 during February and March 1943. Very sadly, he went down with his ship, the "Bonneville" and most of his crew, which I will go into at a later stage.

We had numerous delays on account of fog. There was a count of ships on 4th August, when four ships were reported missing. On 5th August the

Sydney portion and S.C. 39 consisting of 27 ships joined HX 142 until August 13th when S.C. 129 parted company. The Convoy now consisted of 98 ships. The "British Chemist" and the "Baronesa" were in collision in the fog. But only the upper works got damaged and they were able to proceed.

Our escorts were H.M.S. "Ausonia", A.M.C. She joined the Convoy at 09.15 hours on August 2nd. Local escorts were H.M.C.S. "Rosthern" until August 1st. H.M.C.S. "Annaulis" until August 3rd. H.M.C.S. "Collingwood" until August 4th.

The fourth escort group was H.M.S. "Boadicea", "Beagle", "Salisbury", "Heather", "Orchis", "Picotee", "Snowdrop", "Seagull", "Ayrshire", "Arab" and "Norwich City".

Convoy O.N.4 consisted of 55 ships. Commodore G.N. Jones, DSO, Rtd. R.N.R. in "Lorretto". The C.A.M. ship was the "Empire Hudson".

The destinations for Convoy HX 142 were: Liverpool 23, Loch-Ewe 15, Clyde 10, Barry 13, Belfast 3 - total 64.

At 05.56 hours, August 11th 1941, H.M.S. "Bodicea" received a report from the Admiralty that the convoy had been sighted and reported by a U-boat. Probably convoy O.N.4 or O.N.5 and ordered both convoys to alter course to starboard. Destroyers searched the area and dropped depth charges. (No attack on the convoy took place.)

At 06.44 hours, August 11th 1941, H.M.S. "Snowdrop" reported a signal in position 60 degrees 51 minutes north, 16 degrees 34 minutes west, and believed it to be a U-boat. Twenty depth charges were dropped before contact was lost.

August 11th at 10.25 hours when A.A. practice was being carried out with automatic weapons by the convoy, the S.S. "Adula" signalled H.M.S. "Ausonia" by flags, "I require immediate medical assistance". A further signal stated that a naval rating had been accidentally wounded. The speed of the convoy was 7 knots and the length of the columns approximately three miles, so "Ausonia" dropped astern to abreast of S.S. "Adula" and sent a cutter over for the injured seaman for transfer. He died of three bullet wounds to his chest. The burial service was carried out at 11.00 hours on August 12th, colours were half masted in the convoy from 10.30 hours, rehoisted with "Ausonia"'s colours after the burial. "Ausonia" rejoined her station at 11.48 hours.

The Master's report from S.S. "Adula" stated that the seaman, G. Cooper, CJX236423, aged 23, was instructed to clean the Hotchkiss gun after having been fired by A. Smith, naval rating. The gun was left by Smith recocked, reloaded and catch to safe. Cooper had taken the gun out of its stand without removing the ammunition strip. The gun was found partially dismantled with four bullets missing.

H.M.S. "Ausonia" parted company at 19.30 hours. The number of ships present at the final rendezvous

Merchant Navy Memorial, Tower Hill, London

totalled 92 ships. HX 142, 63 ships, and S.C. 39, 29 ships.

H.M.S. "Arrowhead", "Amelia" and "Eyebright" parted company in position 60 degrees 25 north, 24 degrees 45 west, and shaped course for Reykjavic, Iceland. H.M.S. "Ausonia" arrived at Reykjavic at 09.40 hours on August 13th 1941.

August 13th, at 16.00 hours, the Eastbound convoys, HX 142 and S.C. 39

split, by C in C's orders. H.M.S. "Sabre", H.M.S. "Shikari" and H.M.S. "Hebe" and H.M.S. "Hazard" of the first escort group, were attached to the fourth escort group, as escort for the fast convoy.

We continued to plod along at 7 knots. Commodore Vice Admiral Somerville in the "Manchester Exporter" signalled the convoy discipline and station keeping was satisfactory. The voyage home was without incident. On arrival in Liverpool Bay, the "Empire Flame" rocketed her Sea Hurricane away. When we had a C.A.M. ship in the convoy, they gave us a feeling of confidence should any enemy long-range planes appear to start shadowing us. They had no hesitation in rocketing off and doing battle. These R.A.F. Pilots were very brave indeed.

We arrived in Liverpool on September 6th 1941. Our first job was to get all the ammunition stowed away down into the Magazine. Bridge machine-guns lightly greased and covered, likewise the 4" B.L. and the 12 pounder. The D.E.M.S. Officer came aboard and informed us that we would all be taken off the following day to D.E.M.S.'s barracks, Liverpool. We should stow our kit-bags and hammocks, then report to Liver Buildings for our pay and railway warrants. We lost no time in packing our gear!

It was great to have a whole night's sleep as all the way from Halifax we had been on watch and watch (4 hours on and 4 hours off).

On September 7th we had an early breakfast and moved our gear on to the wharf ready for the Naval transport. I went along and paid my respects to Captain Isaacs and our Gunnery Officer, Mr. Derry. Also to Wally, the cook, the Bosun and the sailors. Just imagine- when we stepped ashore that was the first time anyone other than the Master had set foot ashore for 78 days. I just wanted to get home for some decent food and some much needed sleep. I had lost nearly a stone in weight, probably a result of sea-sickness and the food we were served. (Sir William Reardon's ships were not the best of feeders, which was common knowledge among seamen!).

Officers, Crew and Gunners during my service aboard
S.S. "BOTAVON"

Master	Captain H.G. Isaacs
First Mate	A.J. Hooper
Second Mate and Gunnery Officer	B.J. Derry
Third Mate	J.W. Tait
First Radio Officer	S. Purcell
Second Radio Officer	J.S. Sutherland
Third Radio Officer	E.C. Whitehouse
Chief Engineer	M. Baldwin
Second Engineer	T. Snaith
Third Engineer	J. Banks
Fourth Engineer	H.A. Jones
Fifth Engineer	J.N. Russell
Apprentices:	S.C. Clark
	P. Davies
	A. Hill
	C. Morgan
Bosun	J. Blurton
Carpenter	M. Waite
A/B's:	H.A. Day
	A.W. Kimber
	D. Sultana
	B. Lebona
	J. Colbridge
	J. Hollett
Sailors:	G.R. Carr
	W. Holland
	E. Craig
Deck-boys:	G. White
	T. Sharples
	A. Curbishley
Chief Steward	N.G. Masters
Assistant Stewards:	P. Crawley
	P. Saville
Cabin Boy	W. Webber
Chief Cook	L. Stringer
Second Cook	H. Cruff
Galley Boy	W. Malow

DEMS Gunners:

Gunlayer	J. Sparry
Seaman/Gunners:	G. Grassick
	T. Lewis
	B. Lovatt
Maritime Ack/Ack:	H. Crabtree
	R.H. Hutson

Lascar Firemen and Trimmers:

Total = 20

Chapter 4

CONVOY P.Q. 15

I often wondered what happened to "Botavon" whilst I was serving on different Merchant ships after the war. On completion of our Merchant Navy Memorial at Tower Hill, I attended a service there and afterwards decided to stay behind and make a thorough search of all the ships and crews that we lost in that hard fought and most bitterest of wars to stamp out tyranny and dictatorship. I spotted two of the ships that I had served in, so there and then I decided to go along to Kew Records Office and see what I could come up with. I was delighted to discover that "Botavon" had been made Commodore ship for a Russian convoy. It was a proud moment indeed to discover that this rusty old tramp ship that had sailed the oceans of the world for thirty years had such an honour bestowed upon her.

She was built in 1912 by Chas. Connell, Glasgow. Gross tons 5848. Completed as "Indrakuala" for Thos. B. Roydens Indra Line. In 1915 she was acquired when the Royden Fleet joined the Ocean Steam Ship Company, she was renamed the "Eurypylus". In 1938 she was sold to Continental Transit Company and renamed "Trade". In 1939 she was purchased by the Board of Trade and renamed the "Botavon", and managed by Sir William Reardon Smith, Cardiff.

Having been made Commodore Ship, she was sent round to Middlesbrough to load 2,600 tons of Military stores. She was also fitted with extra armament Ack Ack guns, Oerlikons and Marlins. Also extra accommodation for gunners and the Commodore's staff, signallers, etc in readiness for her convoy to Murmansk. Her Master was Captain Smith, son of Sir William Reardon Smith, the owner. From A.D.M/199/172, her armament was 1 4" B.L., 1 12 Pounder, 2 Oerlikons, 20 mm, 2 twin Marlins and 2 single Marlins firing 303s, 3 depth charges, 4 P.A.C.Rockets and Kites.

Convoy P.Q.15 sailed from Reykjavic 26th April 1942. The Commodore was

Captain H.J. Anchor, R.N.R. The Vice Commodore was in the "Cape Race". The Commodore had a staff of six. "Botavon" was the leading ship of the 4th column. Total number of ships in the convoy was 25. Escorts were H.M.S. London (Cruiser), Ulster Queen (Ack Ack ship), Empire Morn (Catapult-Ship). Destoyers H.M.S. Badsworth, Bodicea, Matchless, Somali, Venomous, and a Norwegian Destroyer St. Albans. Submarine Sturgeon was part of the escort from April 28th to May 2nd . H.M.S. London from April 30th to May 1st. H.M.S. Nigeria from April 28th to May 2nd 1942. The Russian ice- breaker Krassin and the Canadian Montcalm on her delivery voyage. H.M.S. King George V was in the covering force and being foggy she had a collision with the Destroyer H.M.S. Punjabi on May 1st 1942 at 13.45 hrs in about 66 degrees N, 8 degrees W. Only the Captain, four Officers and 201 ratings survived. The King George V was damaged by the subsequent explosion of the Punjabi's depth charges (she suffered damage to her bow sections) and had to withdraw and set course for Liverpool where she arrived on May 9th for repairs. She was relieved by H.M.S. Duke of York. The Aircraft Carrier Victorious and the Cruiser H.M.S. Kenya were also escorting and shadowing. American escorts were the U.S.S. Washington, U.S.S. Tuscaloosa, U.S.S. Wichita. U.S. Destroyers Madison, Plunkett, Wainwright and Wilson, and the British Belvoir, Escapade, Faulknor, Hursley, Inglefield, Lamerton, Marne, Martin, Middleton, Oribi and Punjabi. Submarines Sturgeon, Truant and Unison, Polish submarine Jastrzab (later sunk). Norwegian submarine Uredd, Free French submarine Minerve. They all did covering patrols. The convoy arrived at Murmansk on May 5th 1942.

Air attack on convoy P.Q.15. April.30th 1942. The convoy was spotted by a long-range Condor, 250 miles off Bear Island at 22.00 hrs and was attacked by J.U. 88s which was a very poor attack. 3 bombs were dropped, no damage. May 2nd 1942 at 23.40hrs, position 73 degrees 00 N. 20 degrees 22 E, six enemy aircraft attacked, flying in line ahead about 20 ft above the sea. They were Heinkell 111's carrying torpedoes, each aircraft attacking a different column.

Ships of the convoy and escorts opened fire and it was either the gunners of H.M.S. London or the gunners on the "Botavon" that were responsible for destroying one enemy aircraft which crashed into the sea ahead of "Botavon". Sadly, "Botavon" was struck amidships in the after end of No.2 hold. The vessel listed slightly to starboard and began to settle slowly by the head. All the lifeboats were got away and also two rafts. After about half an hour they were all picked up by H.M.S. Badsworth. On boarding Captain Smith discovered that his son was the Navigating Officer. "Botavon" steadfastly refused to sink so H.M.S. Badsworth fired two shells into her. She still refused to sink and "Badsworth" backed in close and fired a depth charge into her. She sank quickly at about 01.30 hrs on May 3rd. Also sank by Ariel torpedoes were the "Cape Corso" and the "Jutland". Position approx. 72 degrees 02 N. 19 degrees 46 E. North West of North Cape. These three Merchant ships totalling 15,000 Reg/tons went down with full cargoes. All were war supplies for the Soviets from England and America. 137 survivors were picked up. The remainder of the convoy made it to Murmansk.

"Botavon" felt very special to me, my first ship. The time I served aboard her taught me the love of the sea and ships, but most of all the comradeship that exists amongst we happy band of men.

Captain Smith and his crew (everyone survived) were landed at Murmansk on May 6th 1942 and were accommodated at an Army Barracks at Viargaru. I understand that the accommodation was disgusting, no sanitary arrangements, and for five days the food consisted of 1 plate of rice three times a day. On May 21st, 33 of the survivors got a passage on H.M.S. Badsworth for the U.K. Meanwhile the cruiser H.M.S. Trinidad, after her damage on March 29th had been temporarily repaired at Murmansk, was able to steam at 18 knots and was ready by May 9th to leave for permanent repair in the United States. Her departure was delayed until May 13th to allow for air reconnaissance, as there were signs of a northward move of German ships at Trondheim. So the remaining 40 of "Botavon"'s crew were sent aboard H.M.S. Trinidad. Rear-Admiral, G.S.18, Rear- Admiral S.S. Bonham-Carter hoisted his flag in Trinidad. The Russians had promised long range fighter escort to a distance of 200 miles from the Murmansk coast, but although the weather was favourable it failed to materialise. On the morning of May 14th 100 miles out, the "Trinidad" was sighted by aircraft and attacked the same evening by 25 dive bombers, J.U.88s and by 10 torpedo bombers Heinkell 111s at 22.45 hrs and was set on fire. She was hit by a bomb and damaged by a near miss. Several fires started which got out of control. After three hours the ship had to be abandoned. She was finally sunk by a torpedo from H.M.S. Matchless at 01.20 hours (See Plot of Action). Very sadly, out of the 40 survivors from the crew of "Botavon", 18 of them went down with "Trinidad". By some error of communication these 18 seamen are listed as going down with the "Botavon", and all their names appear on the Plaque at Tower Hill.

Their names are: M. Ansul, K. Bauer, A. Brotherton, A. Dad, M.A. Golam, S. Graham, A.W. Griffin, A. Gunn, A. Hamid, E. Hawksworth, F. Meah, S. Meah, V.K. Raman, A. Robinson, A. Sebo, E. Ullah, N. Ullah and P. Williams.

Master's Report Ref. A.D.M. 237/166. Convoy.P.Q.15. Captain Smith. We were bound from Reykjavic to Murmansk with 2,600 tons of Military stores. We were armed with a 4", 12 pounder, 2 Oerlikons, 2 Hotchkiss, 2 Twin Marlins, 2 Single Marlins, 4 P.A.C. Rockets, Kites and 3 depth-charges. Some of the confidential books were thrown overboard in a weighted box and others went down with the ship which was finally sunk by gunfire. The numbers of the crew, including Commodore Anchor and his staff of 6, 4 Naval Gunners and 2 Army Gunners, was 73. There were no casualties. We left Reykjavic on April 26th 1942 and proceeded in convoy P.Q. 15. I was Commodore's ship and my position was the leading ship of the 4th column. We proceeded without incident until the 30th of April when the convoy was attacked by enemy aircraft. Three bombs were dropped, but no ships were damaged. The ships of the convoy and our escorts opened fire. We opened fire with every available gun and either H.M.S. London or my ship were responsible for destroying one of the enemy aircraft which crashed into the sea in flames ahead of us.

Nothing further occurred until 23.40 hrs on May 2nd, when in a position 73 degrees N. 20 degrees 22 E, six enemy aircraft were sighted about 1 mile off our starboard quarter. The sea at the time was calm with a wind

S.E. force 2, the weather was fine and the visibility was moderate. We were proceeding at a speed of 8 knots on a course of 090 degrees. The aircraft were flying in line ahead about 20 ft above the sea. They flew along the starboard side of the convoy and then turned and approached the convoy slightly from the starboard bow, each aircraft attacking a different column. I immediately gave the order "Hard to Starboard" in order to bring my ship head on to the attacking aircraft, but before this order could be carried out I saw a torpedo coming towards the ship from the starboard bow. This torpedo, which appeared to circle in towards us, struck my ship amidships in the after-end of No. 2 hold. There was a very loud explosion and a large column of water was thrown into the air, but there was no flame, smoke or smell. The ship listed slightly to starboard and commenced to settle slowly by the head.

We managed to get all four boats away, also two rafts. There were three men on the rafts and the remainder of the crew were in the boats. When I left the ship, the forward well deck was only 1 foot above the water. We were in the boats for about half an hour before we were picked up by H.M.S. Badsworth, and when I got aboard I found that my son was navigator of this ship. As my ship did not appear to be sinking very rapidly, H.M.S. Badsworth fired 2 shells into her, and as she still did not sink, H.M.S. Badsworth backed close in and fired a depth charge under her, after which she sank quickly at about 01.30 hrs on the 3rd May 1942. The visibility was only moderate during the time we were being attacked and the aircraft came upon us very quickly. Two other ships, the "Jutland" and the "Cape-Corso" were also torpedoed and sunk during the time that my ship was attacked.

All the ships in the convoy opened fire and the Russian ice-breaker "Krassin", which was stationed close to us, was so anxious to engage the enemy that they were firing across our Bridge in their eagerness. One aircraft flew across my bows to within 10 ft of the stem and below the fo'castle head, and as it flew across the stern of the "Cape Corso" the aircraft burst into flames and crashed into the sea. The "Cape Corso" and my ship were both firing at this aircraft, and I am not sure which ship was responsible for bringing down the plane. The "Ulster Queen", an A/A ship, was in the centre of the convoy at the time of the attack and was therefore unable to engage the enemy. We proceeded on board H.M.S. Badsworth to Murmansk, where we arrived on the 6th May. On landing we were all put into Russian barracks at Viargaru. The accommodation was very bad with little or no sanitary arrangements. For five days our only food was a plate of rice three times a day. After five days we moved to Murmansk where we remained until the 21st May when we took a passage home in H.M.S. Badsworth and arrived in Londonderry on 30th May. Forty members of my crew were sent on board H.M.S. Trinidad for a passage home and 18 of them lost their lives in the action in which the vessel was lost. During the voyage homeward in H.M.S. Badsworth, the Cam ship "Empire-Morn" sent up her fighter plane during an air attack on our convoy. After destroying an enemy aircraft, the pilot of the fighter aircraft baled out but his parachute failed to open and in consequence this pilot was killed. We picked up his mutilated body and buried him at sea. During the attack on my ship all my crew behaved very well and the gunners also did remarkably fine work with their guns, firing continuously on every possible occasion.

Master's report ends

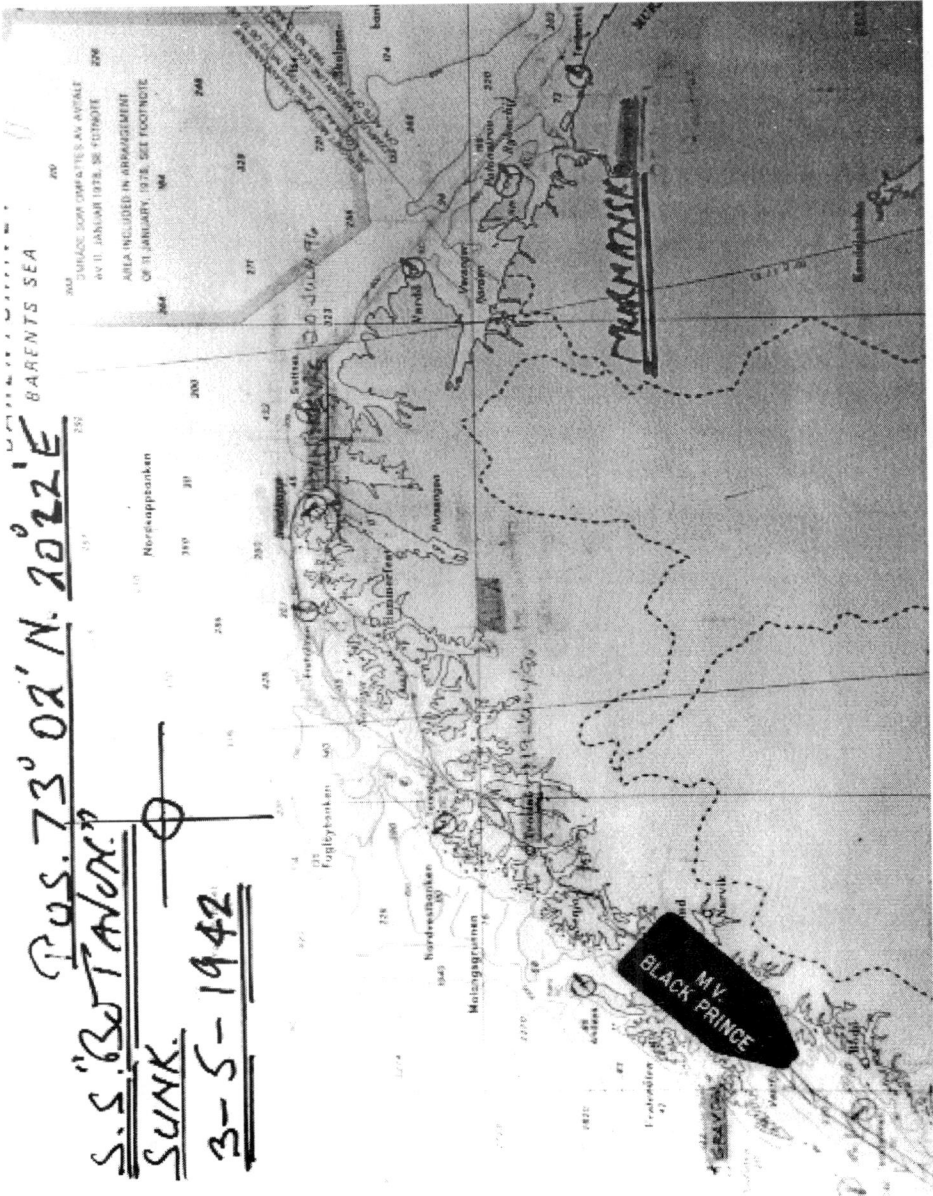

S.S. "BRITTAIN"
Pos. 73° 02' N. 20°22' E
SUNK.
3-5-1942

M.V.PARDO

Built at Harland and Wolff Belfast Yard in1940

Registered Gross tons 5409   Port of Registry Liverpool
number 70888 was sold at the end of the war to Icannista CIA

Nav Pireaus. renamed Aristarchoss

sold for scrap in 1971 ater 31 years of service

Chapter 5

FROM S.S. "BOTAVON" to M.V. "PARDO"

All the D.E.M.S. and Maritime gunners said farewell to "Botavon" on 7th September 1941. We four D.E.M.S. gunners reported to our barracks in Liverpool and stored our kit bags and hammocks. I had a small suitcase, and a kitbag that one of the sailors had made for me. We stayed one night at the barracks and at 09.00 hrs the following morning we reported to The Liver Buildings, collected our back pay, leave allowance and our free railway warrant. A quick good bye and good luck to each other and then for me it was transport to Lime Street station. I was lucky and did not have to wait long for a train to take me across to Chesterfield. Most compartments and corridors were full of servicemen and women. I was lucky enough to get a seat and settled down to catch up with a bit of world news as I had managed to get a paper on the station. It gave me a rough idea as to how the war was going, and the servicemen in the carriage brought me up-to-date with what I did not gather from the newspaper, when I explained that I had been at sea for 78 days and that we were not allowed a radio.

It took about three and a half hours to arrive at Sheffield, and from there I got a connection on a local train to Chesterfield, a distance of roughly fifteen miles. I got a taxi to the bus stop that would take me practically to my doorstep. Then on to a bus and after about fifteen minutes, I was stepping off. There was no charge as the three bus companies were privately owned and I knew them all.

I went round to the back of the farmhouse where we used to take the horses through to the stables, so no one would see me. I had arrived home just at the right time. Everyone had their evening meal at about 5 p.m. I looked through the kitchen window and they were all busy with their meal. I tapped rather heavily on the glass and my Aunt looked up "It's George", she shouted, and just literally bounded out to give me a big hug and kiss. My Uncle was quickly on the scene also Dorothy and Arthur, the Ploughman, Joe, and the maid. They were pleased to see me but "You do look thin", "Whatever have they done to you", were their comments. I told them that I had suffered from seasickness and the food had not been good. My Aunt quickly produced one of her large cups of tea and then went into the big kitchen and reached up and got a ham down off the hook. She cut off a huge thick piece, which easily weighed over a pound, and it almost filled the huge oval cast iron frying pan that was used to cook six eggs at a time. This was, indeed, a treat after the rough food on board ship. An extra large gammon steak cooked in dripping, two fresh eggs and lashings of home made bread and butter and I soon felt a good deal better!

We had lots to talk about. I gave my Aunt the food parcels I had brought from Halifax and she was really pleased. Some duty-free cigarettes and American pipe tobacco for my Uncle were also gratefully accepted. We sat around talking until late and then I went and got some much needed sleep. It seemed quiet not to hear the ship's engines and the dynamo, no movement and no sound of the sea crashing up against the hull of the ship and obscuring the light from the port holes.

All the farmyard noises that I had almost forgotten about after being away at sea for seven months were awakened when the following morning I awoke to the noise of the cows coming in to be milked, horses being fed and harnessed for ploughing, pigs squealing out for their food, cockerels crowing and fighting over who should mate with which hen, and the geese and turkeys making their own kind of sounds.

After breakfast I walked round to the stables and the three horses had not forgotten me - I always used to give them tit bits. Dinah put her nose over the door, snorted with her lips and covered me with spit. Probably her way of saying "Good morning". I spent the next three days visiting relatives, aunts and uncles, and always had a nice welcome.

I had to report back to D.E.M.S. Liverpool on the 17th September, which worked out at 10 days leave. I enjoyed seeing my relatives and old friends and having an up-date on all local gossip. The best part of all was a good nights uninterrupted sleep and some real home cooking. When it was time to leave my Uncle and Aunt took me to the station in their ancient Rover that was used on the milk round. My Aunt's parting instructions were to the effect that when I came on leave in future, I should get a taxi home and she would pay! We did not realise that I would not be having many more leaves.

I got back to Liverpool by noon on the 17th September and was told that I would be joining a ship the following day. No barrack duties so I quickly got round to see some friends who had taken me home when I was doing my gunnery course at HMS Wellesley. My Aunt had packed a dozen eggs in a box for them as a token of appreciation. They were delighted to see me again and wanted to know all about my first ship. We went to a local pub for a drink and to reminisce about the terrible bombing the Liverpudlians had endured. Back home for a fish and chip supper, then farewell and back to barracks.

The following day, 18th September, the Navy transport took me to the docks - although I cannot remember the name - and I joined M.V. "Pardo". The sailor on the gangway directed me to the gunners' accommodation and offered to help with my kit. Accommodation was right aft. One had to go down a flight of stairs and pass the sailors accommodation and mess room to get at ours, which was a continuation through into the tween-decks of number 5 hold. There was accommodation at the rear end of the 4" B.L. gun platform for two in a small cabin with a wash-hand basin.

The Gunlayer in charge, Eric Roberts, a Liverpudlian, was soon on the scene. The other seaman-gunner, Bill Townend, was on leave. After a mug of tea and a smoke Eric took me along to see the Gunnery Officer, Mr. Warren, who was also a Liverpudlian. The Shipping Master was in the saloon signing on a new crew, so I got in the queue. When it was my turn to sign on, the Master, Captain Jones, asked me if this was my first ship. I felt immediately that he would be a very strict Master. My reply was "My second sir, I've just done a trip to Port Sulphur and back here to Liverpool, 78 days without stepping shore". He replied that he had had a few long ones himself. I was told later that he had been in sail so that would account for his brief reply.

My first job was to get acquainted with the armament which was 1 x 4" B.L., 1 Bofor 40 m.m. Ack-Ack, 2 Marlin 303 machine-guns, one on each wing of the bridge, 2 Hotchkis 303 machine-guns, one mounted on each side of the after end of the boat-deck, and smoke floats at the after end of the gun-deck to lay our own smoke screen. I got my kit sorted out and claimed the lower berth. I had to share the accommodation that had been installed for the Army gunners, which consisted of four two-tier bunks with the mess room table in the centre space, the same as my first ship but minus the coal-burning bogey. Instead we had two large steam operated radiators. She was a new ship and had just returned from her first voyage to South America. She was built by Harland and Wolff, Belfast - a beautiful ship and a credit to the ship builders. But I still had a soft spot for my first rusty old tramp-ship.

There were no Army gunners aboard yet so I had my dinner with Eric, in the top cabin at the after end of the gun-deck, which he shared with the other seaman-gunner. Eric had volunteered for the Royal Navy and was a few years my senior. I had smoked all my cigarettes whilst on leave, and to my surprise he gave me a packet of twenty and informed me that he never went short as he used to work for the Imperial Tobacco Company. While Bill was on leave Eric was responsible for the security of the armament and also the magazine. The flooding valve for the magazine was fitted with a lock and the key was kept in his cabin. Someone had to be on duty in case of an air raid or fire. He instructed me in what to do in case of fire in the way of security, and said it would be far better if I stayed in the top cabin and used Bill's berth. The main reason being that the Master would be making his rounds to check that someone was on board. He left me with a liberal supply of cigarettes and said when I went along to get my evening meal I should also get his and it would do for my supper. He then left me to it.

After my evening meal I had a walk round the ship as by this time the dockers had gone ashore. I thought what a very beautiful ship the Irish builders had constructed and I wondered what she would look like in her peacetime livery. I did not know then that my first peacetime ship after the war would be "Pardo"'s sister ship the M.V. "Paraguay", and that she would take me back to all the ports I had been to on my first trip on "Pardo".

("It's a small world" as they say.)

I went up for'ard on the fo'c's'le head and noticed she did not have a 12 pounder Ack-Ack, probably because she had a Bofor 40 m.m. above the 4" B.L. I did not venture onto the bridge as I had noticed that the Master was walking up and down the boat deck. I was later told that he would spend hours pounding up and down the deck.

I had a brief conversation with the A/B on the gangway and then went to my cabin. I was about to turn in when there was a knock on the door. When I opened it there stood the Master. "Good evening, gunner". "Just making sure that someone is aboard in case of fire"! He asked me "Do you know where the control valve is to flood the magazine?" I went over and pointed it out, showed him the lock and where the key was hung in the cabin. He was satisfied and strode away. It was difficult to sleep in a new ship with the different sounds and I was awakened about 6 a.m. by the seagulls on the roof of the warehouse. I was anxious to see what this company served for breakfast, and this proved to be porridge, fish kedgeree, and bacon and egg. I took Eric's along for Bill to make a sandwich when he arrived back from leave. I also collected a loaf of bread which was to last the three of us one day. Eric and Bill had made a small locker to store all the crockery, cutlery, etc. and the condensed milk (we were given one tin per person to last 10 days). One problem on this ship, although she was new, was exactly the same as my first ship, "cockroaches". To stop these loathsome creatures from getting into the milk, we pierced two small holes in the tin, sharpened two pieces of wood to a point and pushed them into the holes. The result was a "cockroach proof" can of 'conny onny' (our name for the condensed milk).

No sooner had I finished my breakfast and washed up then Eric was back aboard. He brought me a morning paper and asked me how I had coped, and asked me if the Master had put in an appearance. I replied "Yes, just before I decided to turn in". He said it was just as well he had pointed out where the flooding valve was for the magazine. He said the Master usually did his rounds every night at about 20.00 hrs. Bill Townend arrived back just before noon. He was from the Isle of Man and was R.N.V.R.

Like me, he was a seaman-gunner and had one good conduct badge for three years service. He was a good shipmate with good sense of humour. The following day we had a visit from the D.E.M.S. Officer, armament inspection followed by a gun-drill. He was satisfied with everything and informed us that the Maritime gunners would be joining us before noon and that we would be sailing in the afternoon for South America.

I went ashore to post my mail and get some razor blades and tooth paste. Bill volunteered to stay aboard to do the security watch for the magazine, so after our meal at 17.00 hrs both Eric and I went ashore. He wanted to see his folks before sailing. I posted my mail and made it to a chemist before closing time. I called in for a pint of good Liverpool ale, collected an evening paper, then back aboard hoping to get a good night's sleep. My hopes were soon dashed, however, when I saw the mattresses that the company had fitted into the steel bunks in the gunners' accommodation. They were what is commonly known amongst seafarers as a "Donkey's Breakfast" which is a sack or bag just long enough to fit the bunk or berth, made out of sacking or burlap, then filled with straw or hay. They used to cost the princely sum of one shilling at the ships' chandlers. The company provided us with one sheet and a pillow case. The straw or hay penetrated the sheet and it was very uncomfortable to ones back and legs. It was one continual prod so I decided to strip my hammock down and cover the "Donkey's Breakfast" with my hammock, then on top of this I laid out the thin mattress that was provided by the Navy, and over this I spread my white naval blanket, half of it to cover the mattress and the other half to wrap over myself. It worked! My half-hour's extra work paid off as I had a good night's sleep!

The following morning I was again awakened by the seagulls on the roof of the warehouse, so I got up. I went up on deck and discovered that Bill was already up before me. We had our breakfast before Eric came aboard. We were soon busy. Our first job was to get all the ammunition belts out of the magazine and take them up on to either wing of the bridge for the Marlin guns, check them both and recover them, then likewise for the two Hotchkis guns on either side of the boat deck. Our next job was to get the four-inch shells up onto the gun deck for the anti-submarine gun mounted on the stern, stow them all in their racks and apply a very light coating of grease, and make sure that the smoke floats were ready to be charged with the "igniter".

We had got everything ready for sea and were having our tea break when the Army gunners arrived. The Sergeant who brought them aboard told them to get their kit below in their accommodation then report back on deck for gun drill. They soon got sorted out. I shared their mess table for my meals. They turned out to be a good team and there were no arguments. We cast off after dark and Eric set the watches. I was 12 - 4 watch but we changed watches every week, which was a good idea and helped to break the monotony,

The weather was kind to me on my first watch but I needed an extra sweater as it gradually got colder before Bill relieved me at 04.00 hrs. We had dropped the Pilot off and were then heading down St George's Channel. The two Maritime gunners got relieved so we three had a mug of tea and a smoke and got turned in. I slept on and off until 08.00 hours, got down for breakfast and then turned in again until 11.00 hours. We had to get our food along at 11.30 to get back on watch at noon. By the time I had had my meal and relieved Eric, I realised that we were out in the open sea – the Atlantic Ocean. I had a quick word with Eric and he handed me a pair of binoculars and told me to keep them round my neck. Also, no smoking on watch as the "Old Man" took a dim view of smoking. As we headed further out into the North Atlantic, the weather steadily got colder so on went the duffel coat and woolly Balaclava. "Pardo" was a fast ship designed to do 15 knots. One of the Engineers told us that they could push her up to 19 knots if we had to outrun a submarine.

The sea began to get choppy and we started to wallow about in the Atlantic rollers. The rain was now coming down heavier than ever. The gun deck was wet all the time so the instinct of self-preservation took over and one had to be careful to keep a good foothold on the slippery wet plates on the gun deck. It seemed to be an eternity before 16.00 hours came round and Bill came out to relieve me. He was a good relief and was always at least 5 minutes early for his watch. We had a quick chat and then I dived below for a long awaited smoke. The heaters were on in the accommodation making a change from the cold gun deck. We did not get our evening meal until 17.00 hours so I decided to slide under the blankets and enjoy a few minutes of joyous agony while the circulation gradually returned to my cold wet body.

The accommodation was stuffy as we had to keep all the portholes clamped down because of the bad weather which was deteriorating all the time. We were beginning to pitch and roll as our accommodation was only just along from the steering-flat, and we also got the noise of the screw when the stern-end lifted out and the propeller blades were just thrashing the air instead. As soon as I had managed to eat my evening meal I clambered back into my bunk as I was not feeling too good. The rolling and pitching gradually intensified and I knew that I was going to be the victim of sea-sickness again. I was not alone as two of the Maritime gunners who were making their first trip kept making a hurried dash to the toilets. The motion on "Pardo" was different to "Botavon" because our accommodation was right aft. On "Botavon" it was practically amidships, all we appeared to be doing was roll fairly heavily, which meant that one had to really jam oneself into the steel bunk the best one could or get catapulted out on to the deck, which one of the first trip Maritime gunners did and severely bruised himself by colliding with the mess-room table.

I got accustomed to the roll, but when the stern-end rose up out of the sea she appeared to stay out for a few moments then come crashing down again with such force it made your stomach want to turn over or seek refuge in your mouth. The only thing I could think to do was to go along and see the chief cook before breakfast and ask him if I could have some rice with curry, this I knew would help settle my stomach. I did manage to doze off and on, and when Eric came down to call me to get on watch at midnight he informed me that it was sea boots and oilskin weather.

When I made it up on to the gun deck it was as black as the hobs of hell and raining very heavy. There was a mug of tea waiting for me but I only took a few sips and then flung it over the side for I knew that it would not stay down very long. It turned out to be one long cold wet miserable four hours, as I tried to penetrate and peer into the jet blackness of the night searching for ships or submarines. It crossed my mind to wonder how submarines managed to operate in these appalling conditions. No one had told me how they did. This being only my second trip I was still a bit of a greenhorn! I was to find out later, much to my horror, that the German U-Boats could and did operate under these and much worse conditions. Gale force ten was no problem to them as I was to discover in a later eastbound convoy across the North Atlantic.

Bill relieved me early. He knew that I had not fully recovered from my bouts of seasickness, so just a quick "Nothing to report" and a quick exit from the gun deck, then down below to my bunk. I wedged myself in and slept until 07.30 hrs to be awakened by the Army gunners having their breakfast. I decided to get up and go along and see the chief cook. I told him about my problem and he said "Not to worry son - come along every morning and I will give you a large plate of boiled rice mixed with curry while the bad weather lasts". It did not present much of a problem as this company, "The Royal Mail Lines" had fish kedgeree on their breakfast menu every day. This kept me going and I could always keep it down. There is something to be said for curry as an aid for mal de mer.

The weather and sea were getting friendlier towards me day by day and we were able to open all the portholes in the accommodation. Everywhere needed a good airing after days and days of bad weather and being battened down. We tried to get rid of the smell of wet duffel coats being dried out on the radiators, along with the smell of tobacco smoke, although fortunately we only had one pipe smoker. The smell of unwashed and scruffy bodies was another noticeable feature. Two of the Army gunners did not know what soap looked like and were not shaving until Eric had a word with their Lance Corporal. He told them to make good use of the showers and get shaved, wash their stinking clothes and bloody well smarten themselves up. Something that they had not known about was the Master's Inspection every day (other than Sunday). All bunks had to be made up, although anyone coming off watch at 08.00 hrs and turned in after breakfast was excused and could stay in their bunk. Captain Jones did not miss a thing and was very quick to draw attention to any form of untidiness or a badly cleaned wash room. There was no excuse as we drew a weekly allowance of hard soap from the chief steward for scrubbing out. Everyone took a turn at scrubbing out and for getting the food along.

I was now able to tackle my food and enjoy it - best of all I could once again enjoy a cigarette, although I preferred to roll my own. The sailors on my first ship had taught me the knack - if there is one. I did buy a cheap pipe and a four-ounce tin of St. Bruno from the steward but discovered it appeared to burn my tongue so I stowed it away in my kit bag. Hopefully, I would be able to take it home and give it to Freddy Gray. He was a tough old coal miner who had survived thirty years of hacking away at the coal face for a mere pittance of a wage and he had promised to look after our garden until I returned home.

The first really warm weather had now arrived and the sea had flattened itself out to a long lazy swell. We could sit around on number five hatch, telling yarns and smoking. Everyone smoked in those days, non-smokers were a rare breed of seaman, and, needless to say, so were non-drinkers. Suddenly the alarm bells rang for action stations, gun crews and fire fighting parties, no one excused, everyone had to be present at his allotted station. I was number two on the 4" gun, strap a belt of percussion tubes round my waist, open the breach ready to receive the four-inch shell. After the shell was rammed home the cordite charge was loaded, then I had to close the breech with the percussion tube in and shout "ready". (The shell was not used during practice or the cordite charge because once the shell had been rammed home, the gun had to be fired as the copper band on the shell would have been hard up into the rifling of the barrel.) The Gunnery Officer having satisfied himself that both gun crews had been up to standard, dismissed us, as did the Chief Officer with his fire fighting parties.

The Master, having stood us down, gave us the opportunity to get to know each other. The sailors who made up the rest of the gun crew had all attended gunnery school at various ports around the coast to learn how best to defend their ship. Their lot had been the same as ours during the severe weather we had encountered. Come off watch, have a meal and get turned in - the only place where one gained a small respite from the elements.   Sleep, read and smoke if one could.   The Bosun, Mr Jackson (or "Jacko" as he was known) was still busy seeing that all the fire hoses had been draped over the derricks at number 4 and 5 hatches to get dried out before being stowed in their red Fire Boxes. Chippy, the ship's carpenter, was making sure that the canvas covers from the ventilators and the smoke helmet and pump were safely stowed away

Mr. Dingle was like the Master, one of the old school of merchant seamen, very pre-war. He sported a huge bushy black beard, out of which pro-truded a large and expensive Dunhill pipe; he was never without it when he was making his rounds and he had a great sense of humour. One of the sailors, Jimmy O'Callagan, said "Sir, is it true that you had to get the Chippy to cut off your white sea boots?" After a week of heavy weather that we had passed through, he never slept in his bunk but on his settee with his huge white fisherman's trawler-type sea boots on.   Not to be outdone, Mr. Dingle replied "O'Callagan, if you stay in this company till the end of the war I will donate them to you". Poor Jimmy, we did not know at the time that he would not be with us much longer. The day after we had our action stations and fire drill, all the Officers changed into their white tropical rig.   So we Navy and Maritime gunners did likewise.

I got to know all the sailors and the engine-room hands, greasers and wip-ers.   Now the hot weather was with us all the time, everyone used to congregate on the after end of number 5 hatch.   We smoked endless cigarettes and swapped stories. The main topic was where we were go-ing, what country and what port.   Everyone knew that we had loaded a cargo for South America. We were well south of the Azores and the sail-ors coming down from the bridge would say South by West, or we are still on a southerly course. We must be going through the Caribbean to Panama, then through the Canal and across the Pacific to Australia. However, to dispel all the wild guesses and rumours, Eric, the carpenter, said he and the two cadets had been down Number 1 & 2 holds to shore up some cargo that had come adrift, and everything was stamped or stencilled for ports in South America, i.e. Rio de Janeiro, Santos, Montevideo, and Buenos Aires. That completely scuppered everyone's guesswork.   Bill Townend then told everyone what we gunners already knew and what the D.E.M.S. Officer had told us, that we would be sailing for South America.

We arrived at the port of Trinidad during the early hours of Sunday morning and dropped anchor. Here we had to wait until Monday morning for the water and oil barges to come out and top us up, not forgetting the Chief Steward's stores of fresh vegetables (the old "spud locker" on the after end of the boat deck was looking very sad after our long haul across the North Atlantic from Liverpool!). We heard that the Master would be going ashore before noon Monday to the ships' agents as we did not know whether or not we would be proceeding on our own again down into the South Atlantic. So what do we do on a Sunday swinging round the anchor and with no radio as we were not allowed to have one? Only one thing to do, get stuck into our dhobying, stretch a line between the derricks on number 5 hold and give all our gear a good airing and drying in the hot tropical sun, instead of the pokey little drying room that was shared by the gunners, sailors, greasers and cleaners. Having done this we just waited and hoped that when the Master came back aboard there would be some mail from home.

We were soon galvanised into action by Enoch. He was one of the sailors, a cockney and a real old shellback who had gone ashore in June 1939. As soon as war was declared he came back to sea again. He was a mine of information on ships, ports and foreign shores. On this occasion he came up from the accommodation with an assortment of fishing lines and hooks. I can't recall what he used for bait to catch the first fish, but whatever kind it was it was immediately cut up and used to bait all the remaining hooks. Various fish were caught and hauled aboard onto the wooden deck. Someone had hooked a small Hammerhead shark, which I had never seen before. I could see why it had been so aptly named. The large hammer shaped parts that stuck out on either side also contained its eyes. I could imagine what a very large one would look like. I hooked a small octopus and was interested in its shape and movements until it decided to attach its suckers to my arm. It felt most uncomfortable - perish the thought of becoming entangled with the extra big ones that had frequently sunk ships. Bill Townend helped me to prize it off, and Enoch cut it up for more bait. Jimmy O'Callagan landed a fairly large fish, about 18" long, which I was told was a catfish. However, while Jimmy was unhooking it it somehow speared his wrist with what appeared to be a long thin piece of white bone. It snapped off so we got Mr Warren, who was in charge of the Medicine locker, to come along and look. We did not carry a doctor on board. The piece of catfish bone was removed from Jimmy's arm and then bandaged. We were then advised not to land catfish as their spike was poisonous.

Later, Enoch appeared with his well worn "squeeze box" and we sat around on the after No. 5 hatch and had a really good sing-song, sea shanties, rude songs and war time songs and our morale was very high. It is surprising what a good sing-song does for one. We also got a couple of bottles of beer each. We were allowed a daily beer ration at the discretion of the Master and depending on supplies. Unfortunately, we Navy and Army gunners could not afford this every day!

There was much concern on Monday as Jimmy's wrist was very inflamed and swollen. He went ashore with the Master's launch when it called round to collect him. They both arrived back at noon and the sad story was that Jimmy's wrist was poisoned by the catfish and he had to sign off to get professional medical treatment ashore. We were sorry to see him leave as he was a good pre-war sailor.

After the launch took Jimmy ashore we upped anchor and headed southwards into the South Atlantic and our first port was Rio de Janeiro. This was the first time for me and the Army gunners. What a magnificent sight it was, a large bay, part of which was the famous Cococabana beach or millionaires playground, the Sugar Loaf mountain was aptly named as we saw as soon as it came into view on our port side and reared itself majestically skywards. Further to the back of the Sugar Loaf and situated on a small plateau was the Cocovado – this was the famous sculpture made out of marble of the Christ. It was immense and appeared to be at least 40 to 60 feet in height. At night it was illuminated, making it an excellent landmark for navigators arriving after sunset.

The normal procedure for all gunners about to enter port was carried out. Belts of ammunition stowed away and all guns covered and lashed down. We had an early visit from the R.N. D.E.M.S. Officer. He was in civvies and had us all mustered down below on the mess-deck. He informed us most emphatically not to go ashore in our Navy or Army uniforms. Brazil was a neutral country and if we wore our uniforms we would probably be arrested. After he had shot off down the gangway there was a rush to sort out our civilian clothes. Both Eric and Bill had been here on a previous voyage so they took me along with them to show me around. We had a special roster when in port which ensured that there was always two gunners aboard in case of fire to flood the magazine. I was greatly impressed by the shops in Rio de Janeiro. We stopped at a bar to try the local beer, peanuts and hardboiled eggs.

We took a half-day off and paid a visit to Cococabana beach, the largest beach I had seen to date and there was no shortage of good looking young ladies soaking up the sun. The shops along the sea front were stocked with souvenirs, making it difficult to decide what to buy. After much deliberation I bought a pretty veneered wooden tray depicting a scene of the harbour, mountain and the lovely Cocovado. We still use this today, after 57 years.

From Rio we sailed further south to the port of Santos where we managed to get a friendly game of soccer against a Norwegian ship and we held them to a draw. This port was not quite as colourful as Rio de Janeiro. We stayed here for four days, then sailed to Montevideo where we had to anchor out and wait for a pilot to take us up to Buenos Aires. The German pocket battleship had been scuttled in the harbour after having fought a losing battle with H.M.S. Ajax, Achilles and Exeter. Her fighting top was still visible, about 30 feet of it above the water. I managed to get a photograph of it. The pilot came aboard and took us up to Buenos Aires during daylight hours. A very colourful city. Seeing all the city lights as darkness fell was a welcome sight after the rigorous blackouts back home. We managed to spend a few hours at the Mission to Seamen, which was run by an English Padre who organised a dance for us. We were not allowed to escort the girls home, but we appreciated their company. Before we left the Padre provided us with quite an assortment of both books and magazines for which we were very grateful. Our ship did not have a library – probably it was being used as an ammunition locker.

A couple of days before we sailed the Chief Steward enquired of all the crew and gunners if we wanted him to order tins of "Extracto-de-carne" for us. This was meat extract, a by-product of the numerous canning factories that turned out cans of corned beef which, incidentally, was to be the bulk of our cargo for the U.K. I had heard about this from others who had made previous visits. It was much like Bovril and made a good hot drink during cold weather. We also had the opportunity to buy 5lb tins of corned beef to take home.

It was soon time to cast off and head back to Montevideo. We had loaded a mixed cargo from Rio de Janeiro, Santos and Buenos Aires, the bulk of it being tinned food. We could not load bulk carcasses of beef as we were not a refrigeration ship, that was left to the ships owned by Lord Vesty, the big "Blue Star" ships and also the big ships owned by Houlder Brothers, and any refrigeration ships that had joined us when their countries had been overrun by the Nazis.

We dropped the Pilot off at Montevideo, took one last look at the German pocket-battleship "Graff-Spee" that had lain there since she was scuttled on the orders of Hitler December 17th 1939, and headed out to sea on our own and set course for England. It felt strange putting out to sea on our own after having been in convoys - the only consolation being that we had the speed to outrun a German submarine. No chance though against an armed raider or German pocket battleship, so out into the great expanse of the unknown, keep an extra sharp lookout and hope for the best. The weather stayed reasonably good until we were abeam of the Canary Islands, then it started to deteriorate quickly. Much to my disappointment and embarrassment, I was once again seasick, although not as bad as when I was on the "Botavon". I knew that I would overcome this eventually.

On the 7th December, news came down from the bridge that the Japanese had entered the war in a most disgraceful and cowardly manner, by attacking the greater part of the American Navy while it lay at anchor in Pearl Harbour. The Day of Infamy. This finally brought the Americans into the war against the Axis powers. Up until this time they had driven some very hard bargains as we are all well aware, with their Lease Lend policies which are far too numerous to name. Mr. Roosevelt did make the most rude and unforgivable remark on one occasion to his cronies during a discussion about Lease Lend, which was "England is a big fat cow and we will milk her till her tits are dry". It was a most disgusting remark to make as we had stood alone since September 1939 - that is two years and three months of blood, sweat and tears. Our Merchant Navy being decimated day by day by U-Boats, surface raiders and Pocket Battleships, and anything else that Donetze wanted to throw at us. Our cries for help always fell on deaf ears time after time. We sailors were all sorry for the wives, parents and relatives of those who died at Pearl Harbour at the hands of the Japanese. One thing that we all agreed on was that the tide would now turn in our favour. There were no blackouts in America - Nazi bombers could not reach their shores - so there was round the clock production of munitions. We are all quite aware that without Uncle Sam we would have lost this most horrendous of wars.

We arrived back in Liverpool on December 9th. While we were stowing the ammunition away I was at the bottom of the magazine shaft passing the 4"shells through to my mate inside the locker. One shell toppled off the tray and hurtled down about six feet. Luckily I managed to grab it with both hands, and although it had a thin coating of grease I broke its fall and it landed base upwards on my left foot. These shells weigh a little over 60lbs and it gave me quite a jolt. I realised that my big toe had taken the brunt of the impact. I refused to send the tray back up until I had been relieved, which did not take long as everyone wanted to get the ammo stored away so we could get home on leave. I went to find the Second Mate and Gunnery Officer, Mr Warren, who also acted as ships' doctor. He was busy putting his charts away and when I told him what had happened he remarked "Well gunner, it's a damn good thing it did not fall nose down or the ship would have been blown up". After this incident, the tray was deemed to be unsafe and before we sailed again it was replaced with a tray that had sides and were built up higher than the total length of the shells so that they could not topple over.

My toe was in a mess but was soon cleaned up. By this time all the ammo had been stowed away and the hatch locked. The D.E.M.S. Officer came aboard and was in good spirits when he was informed that all the guns had been covered and secured and all the ammo stored away.

The good news was that we three D.E.M.S. gunners would not be taken off and put into barracks but would be going on leave and should report back. All the Army gunners left by truck. It was really excellent news that we were to stay in the same ship as we were a good team and she was a happy ship. Most important she had the speed. I reported in at Liver Buildings to collect my leave allowance and also my free railway warrant. I got away on December 10th and was told to report back on board on December 18[th,] which gave me 8 days leave. I got a train departing before noon and if my connections went off without a hitch I would, hopefully, arrive home in time for tea. I could not phone ahead as telephones were a luxury that most farmers could ill afford. When I got to Chesterfield, I took a taxi and was home in time for tea. I gave the family the presents that I had brought back, not forgetting my chocolate ration that I had saved for the children. I had a good leave meeting relatives and friends and I reported back to my ship on the morning of the 18th.

On the 20th December we sailed round to Newport to the ammunition wharf and commenced loading at all five holds - cargo various for Singapore. The Master instructed Eric that half of the gunners could have a 72 hour pass to enable them to have Christmas at home. We drew lots and I was one of the lucky ones to get a 72 hour pass and railway warrant. I had two days at home – this was to be my last visit home for 15 months. I reported back to my ship on time. Bill Townend had been posted to another ship so I was back in the two berth cabin situated abaft the 4" gun deck. On the 4th January we sailed from Newport via Barry Road to Greenock, where a large fleet of Merchant ships and Troop ships were assembling.

While at Newport, the Master received Admiralty cipher message dated 3.1.42. Reads "Intend sailing "Pardo" from Barry Roads at 12.00 hrs 4.1.42.escorted by H.M.S. Vanoc, and also Fighter Protection. E.T.A. Greenock 16.00 hrs 5.1.42." H.M.S. Vanoc ordered to rendezvous with "Pardo" at 14.30 hrs at Scarweather and escort her to the Clyde. Second A.D.M. cipher message. "Intend to sail Clyde portion of convoy W.S.15. Vessels including "Pardo" to pass the Clyde Boom at 21.30 hrs on 10.1.42."

We arrived at Greenock at 16.00 hrs 5.1.42. At the assembly point there was quite a lot of movement going on, troopships and cargo ships looking for suitable anchorage. This aroused a lot of interest as most of us had never seen so many large ocean-going passenger ships stripped of all their lovely peace-time colours and covered from stem to stern and truck to keel in drab wartime grey. No sooner had we dropped the anchor, than a boat arrived alongside with a working party of carpenters and a foreman with a load of timber. The ship's gangway was quickly lowered for them to board. The sailors had two derricks rigged and the timber was landed on top of number 5 hold.

The carpenters went about the job of constructing temporary accommodation in the tween decks in the after end of number 5 hold on the port side. This was to accommodate fourteen soldiers who, we discovered later, were bound for Singapore. It was very soundly constructed and they had their own mess room arrangements to tend for themselves, as did our Army gunners. The carpenters constructed their own entrance via a flight of thick broad stairs and a cleverly designed "Scuttle-Hatch" complete with doors and a blackout curtain. The gunner who replaced Bill Townend was another seaman-gunner, this was his first ship. He took rather a dim view at having to share accommodation with the Army Bofors gunners, but as I pointed out I had to share for three months and they turned out to be good mates. His name was John Withell. On the morning of 10th January 1942, the Navy launch collected the Master, and also the Masters from the troopships and supply ships, to receive their sailing orders. He was back before noon. Our sailing orders were to up anchor and pass the "Clyde Boom" at 21.30 hrs on 10th January 1942.

Commodore Ship   "Strathmore"
Commodore   A.T. Tillard, D.S.O., R.N.R.
Convoy consisting of 16 troopships and 7 store ships full with supplies
ESCORTS:

         H.M.S. Resolution (Battle ship)
         H.M.S. Cheshire
         H.M.S. Ascania
         H.M.S. Vanquisher
         H.M.S. Norman
         H.M.S Boreas
         H.M.S. Skate

H.M.S. Wirorn
H.M.S. Heemskerk
H.M.S. Blyskawica
H.M.S. Antony
H.M.S. Witherington
H.M.S. Volunteer
H.M.S. Garland
H.M.S. Vanoc
H.M.S. Warker
H.M.S. Verity
H.M.S. Columbia (Submarine Depot Ship)

On January 16th extra Destroyers joined us:
H.M.S. Wivern
H.M.S. Demi-Hissar
Troopships and Store Ships. Speed to be maximum 15 knots. Average speed to be12 to 13.5 knots. 4 Cables between columns and 3 Cables between ships.

TROOPSHIPS
Llangibby-Castle. (Suffered U-Boat damage.)
Pasteur.
Staffordshire
Strathmore
Strathnaver
Viceroy of India
Brittanic
Stirling Castle
Chaistzam
Huygens
Laconia
Empire-Woodlark
Arawa

Letita
Orontes
Otranto

STORE-SHIPS
Autolycus
Aagtekerk
Port Chalmers
Pardo (my ship)
Dorset
Elizabeth Bakke
Melbourne Star

Our first and most important duty was to get the machine-guns on the bridge and boat-deck uncovered and loaded, and the safety catches on. Get the 4" shells up from the magazine and also the 40 m.m. shells for the Bofor gun. During our stay in Liverpool, the Chief Officer had made sure that the magazine hoist had been modified to prevent any further shells hurtling down the magazine shaft and squashing someone's foot, as happened to me.

The extra fourteen soldiers who were en route for Singapore were busy getting familiarised with the ship, as none of them had been on a Merchant ship before. Most of the crew of regular Merchant seamen had signed on again, the Bosun, the Carpenter Eric, and the Engine room storekeeper, Billy Mcquillan, who used to get stewed out of his mind when in port. It was good to see Enoch back again with his "squeeze box". As soon as the guns had been made ready for action, watches were set 4 hours on and 8 hours off. The Master had told Eric to work out a watch keeping roster to include all the soldiers we now had aboard, for the more look-outs we had the better. An extra roster was made out for the soldiers and I took it down below and pinned it up in their quarters. I said "There you are mates - keep an extra sharp look out as I have seen what has been loaded and should we get hit we have all the ingredients for a major catastrophe". A united chorus went up of "Just what is down there?" I replied "Sorry chaps - just make sure you keep a sharp look out" and left them to it.

We set the watches – Eric took the 4-8, Johnny the 8-12, and I did the 12-4. The course took us down the Firth of Clyde, passing the boom at 21.30 hours 10th January 1942, into the North Channel and rendezvous with the Liverpool portion of the convoy. Troopships: "Empire-Woodlark", "Arawa", "Letita", "Orontes", "Otranto". Storeships: "Melbourne Star" and "Elizabeth Bakke". Escorts: H.M.S. Vanquisher, H.M.S. Volunteer, H.M.S. Boreas, H.M.S. Witherington, H.M.S. Demi-Hissar, and O.R.P. Garland, from Londonderry at 10.30 hours 11th January 1942. In position 270 degrees. Oversay 16 miles. Speed to rendezvous 10 knots, then advance to 13 knots. Then out into the North Sea.

We experienced quite a lot of bad weather during which some of the cargo in the tween decks at number 5 hold moved port side and stoved in the new accommodation where the soldiers were housed. Fortunately, there were no casualties. Chippy got busy, assisted by some of the sailors, and they made a good job of shoring up the damaged sections. It was earmarked for reconstruction at the first port of call.

I was beginning to overcome my seasickness and after my meal it was straight into my bunk. It had its advantages sharing the cabin abaft the gun deck as it saved time reaching action stations. Three of the new Army gunners had also gone down with seasickness. This is pretty unpleasant when so many men are sharing fairly small accommodation. The soldiers travelling to Singapore were also under the weather but their Officer administered brandy and this gave them some relief. As soon as we entered calmer waters, action stations was sounded – it was time for gun drill and fire drill. We were kept at it until Mr. Warren and Mr. Dingle were satisfied that we were up to standard!

The convoy was very well formed and the station keeping first-class now that we had left the bad weather astern of us. The large troopships and supply ships presented a magnificent sight. The most impressive sight of all was the Battleship H.M.S. Resolution, along with her escorts. On Sunday morning she had a full Marine band standing atop of one of her forward turrets dressed in their full tropical rig with "Pith helmets". They played a medley of tunes whilst steaming up and down the columns. Just imagine the excitement that was generated amongst the troops and sailors lining the rails – it made us feel very proud to be

British.

The following is taken from the official files at Kew Records Office

14 January 1942. ADM/199/1211. Admiralty informed me that "U" boats might be in vicinity of rendezvous "X" and amended the rendezvous to 2Y2 (47 degrees 20' N, 18 degrees W) at 1000Z/15th January. A D/F bearing of a "U" boat transmission obtained by "Anthony" agreed with this. The Admiralty further ordered that "Resolution" was to remain north and east of the rendezvous until that time and gave a subsequent route to be followed thereafter.

Late in the evening, a position course and speed report was received from "Vanquisher", who was Senior Officer of the A/S escort attached to the convoy.

15 January 1942. Admiralty amended position of rendezvous "Y" to 48 degrees 40' N; 18 degrees W. This was exactly that position which would be reached at the appointed time by the convoy if "Vanquisher's" report was correct. It is thought, however, that like "Resolution" she had been in a gale without sights for some days.

This signal was received at 04.30 (Zone + 1) and involved an immediate alteration of course accompanied by an increase to more than full speed for the rendezvous to be punctually effected. "Anthony", on the screen, had, however, lost touch during the night, partly because her R.D.F. set broke down. It was therefore necessary to continue on the same course and speed until "Norman" fetched her back after daylight.

Course was then altered so as to join the convoy at 13.00 but nothing was sighted, although it was continued until 14.00.

The heavy sea still prevailing limited "Resolution's" speed to 15 knots and a long stern chase after the convoy was to be avoided. It was therefore necessary at 14.00 to order her to steer similar courses and speeds to the convoy. The difficulty of finding even a convoy in dull and heavy weather, when unwilling to break W/T silence to ascertain its position, was thus fully experienced, and it was not till dusk that a signal made by "Vanquisher" indicated that the convoy had been four and a half hours late in passing through the rendezvous.

At dusk this evening O.R.P. "Garland" was detached to continue on her passage to Gibraltar.

16th January. In the forenoon an Admiralty signal was received to the effect that convoy W.S.15 was being reported by a "U" boat. It was therefore unquestionably best to hold off "Resolution" from junction with the convoy until daylight the next day. This course of action was successfully taken. Meanwhile, shortly after receipt of this Admiralty signal, O.R.P. "Garland" reached the prudent limit of her outgoing endurance and simultaneously S.S "Llangibby Castle" (one of the convoy) reported herself as being bombed. "Garland" was therefore directed to part company, investigate, take any necessary action, and then return to her home base. She, in fact, found the convoy but not "Llangibby Castle" and was informed that the latter was steering by engines at 12 knots for the next lettered position on the convoy route.

An hour or more after "Garland" had been detached a message was received from "Boreas" stating that at 09.00 "Llangibby Castle" had been hit by torpedo. The evidence then before me, therefore, was that "Llangibby Castle" had been both torpedoed and then bombed. Indeed, though the ship was, I now know, making 10 knots until her arrival at Horta, Azores, I am still uncertain of the truth of the reported bombing or of its accuracy if bombing there was.

The afternoon was enlivened by Admiralty signals that an enemy aircraft was presumed to be homing 3 "U" boats onto the convoy, which was ordered to proceed at utmost convoy speed. The enemy aircraft was, in fact, seen from "Resolution", but out of range. Meanwhile, "Resolution" and escort were kept in pace with it on the presumed safer side and throughout the night kept station thereon by R.D.F. Type 273.

17 January. At daylight took station in convoy W.S.15 abreast S.S. "Strathmore", the Commodore's ship, and learnt from him:

(a) that S.S "Aagtekerk" was standing by S.S "Llangibby Castle". (At the convoy conference she had been detailed as the correct rescue ship to do so.)

(b) that M.V. "Pardo" (storeship) had had to heave to. (The new accommodation in the tween deck was stoved in.)

(c) that Asdics of the "Demi-Hissar" (a destroyer of the escort) were not working.

The convoy present, therefore, consisted of twenty ships in six columns with "Resolution", "Cheshire", "Ascania" and H.M.N.S. "Heemskerk" as an additional column near the centre. As A/S escort there were "Norman" (S.O.), "Boreas" and "Demi-Hissar". Considerations of the fuel required to return home had caused the other destroyers formerly attached to part company on the previous day in accordance with their original instructions.

It was now time to consider the fuelling of H.M.N.S. "Heemskerk" and the A/S Escort at Ponte Delgada, and it became apparent that if only one ship were to be away at a time, then the last one to be detached would have not only a two days' trip north but would also fail to regain the convoy before Freetown.

At 15.20 therefore, the positions of all reported "U" boats being well astern, "Boreas" and "Demi-Hissar" were detached for Ponte Delgada and H.N.M.S. "Heemskerk" and "Norman" became the A/S screen. "Heemskerk" immediately reported that she was not fitted with Asdics, but took no exception to the reply that it was hoped the "U" boats would not know it.

18 January. Wind southerly – still a head wind – but now reduced to force 6. M.V. "Pardo", who had become detached when she hove to some days back, now rejoined.

(Note: This was after the Chippy, the Bosun and sailors had shored it up. There were no casualties amongst the soldiers.)

From early p.m. until next morning, a succession of W/T messages in plain language variously addressed by S.S. "Llangibby Castle" were intercepted. She first gave her position, course, and speed (10 knots) and requested a tug from Horta, Fayal. She next asked Horta W/T whether navigation lights on Fayal Island were burning at full power, and later told a foreign merchant ship of her damage and position and that she hoped to arrive Horta at daylight. Further signals of the same nature followed; nevertheless, S.S. "Llangibby Castle" reached harbour without suffering further attack.

In the afternoon, H.M.N.S. "Heemskerk" was detached for fuel and after dark "Norman" similarly parted company.

19 January.   "Boreas" rejoined but "Demi-Hissar" had sustained damage to her stem in Ponte Delgada harbour and it was learnt that the necessity for repair locally had prevented her from sailing until 19th January.

20 January. On return from oiling "Norman" again took up her A/S screening station. Later H.M.N.S. "Heemskerk" also rejoined.

21 January. In the afternoon, "Vansittart", who had been despatched from Freetown by Commander-in-Chief, South Atlantic, joined company and reinforced the A/S screen.   She reported one engine out of action and her maximum speed as 22 knots.

After nightfall, "Resolution" was ordered to proceed ahead of the convoy to effect an ocean rendezvous with the oiler R.F.A. "Rapidol" which had been arranged for 08.00 next day.

On sailing from the United Kingdom it had been hoped that the passage to Freetown would be effected without the necessity for fuelling en route but the continuous heavy weather from ahead during the first six days at sea had caused such hopes to be disappointed.

22 January. "Resolution" met R.F.A. "Rapidol", accompanied by "Jasmine" as her escort, and attempted to take in fuel by "T" method (two ways) and by the oiler towing from ahead.   In the strong trade wind conditions (wind force 6) all attempts were unsuccessful.

The fuel situation was now becoming serious. The amount left in "Resolution" would not allow her to proceed appreciably south of Bathurst and at that place shoal water would force the ship to lie in the open swell several miles from the coast. The decision was therefore taken to shape course for Murdeira Bay, Sal Island, in the Cape Verde Group and to try again, either off Sal Island or in Murdeira Bay. If once more unsuccessful, Bathurst could still be reached.

23 January. At 08.30 in the lee of Sal Island, just outside territorial waters, the wind and sea were still too great for oiling at sea to be accomplished with any speed, so proceeded into Murdeira Bay where "Resolution" anchored at 09.22 and R.F.A. "Rapidol" immediately came alongside. Meanwhile, "Vansittart" and "Jasmine" acted as A/S Screen in the approaches to the bay.

Oiling ceased at 12.30 and "Rapidol" cast off from alongside and anchored clear so that "Vansittart" could now fuel. "Jasmine" continued to act as A/S Screen in the entrance.

It was judged that the greater safety for "Resolution" now lay in her proceeding to sea and zigzagging at moderately high speed. The ship therefore proceeded at 18 knots, shaping a mean course for Freetown and "Vansittart" was told to rejoin as A/S Screen at daylight the next morning. As the bay was cleared a small boat flying a large Portuguese flag was observed pulling out from the shore. It was later learnt that the boat contained a Customs Authority and the Chief of the Administration from Santa Maria, the largest settlement on the island. They wished to know the reason and length of the visit, were very pro-British and did not express any resentment at the arrival of H.M. Ships. Names of ships were not given but the usual customs forms were completed for "Vansittart" and "Rapidol".

24 January. "Vansittart" was for some reason not in sight at daylight. "Resolution's" position, course, and speed were therefore passed by W/T to her. Meanwhile, the Commander-in-Chief, South Atlantic, offered the service of two escort vessels from Bathurst for a period. Calculation showed that these ships could not reach "Resolution" until off the approaches to Freetown and advantage was therefore not taken of this offer. Convoy W.S.15 was due to enter Freetown at 11.00 next day and at dusk "Vansittart" had not rejoined. Commander-in-Chief, South Atlantic, was therefore requested to send back a destroyer, when available, to escort "Resolution".

25 January. In response to this request "Vimy" joined company at 08.30. Two hours later "Vansittart" also joined "Resolution's" A/S Screen. Her tardy arrival was explained as due to an incorrect estimation of the speed the ship could do on one engine.

At 13.30 "Resolution" entered the swept channel and anchored off Freetown at 17.05. **ends**

This would be the day "Pardo" arrived at Freetown.

We arrived at Freetown after H.M.S. "Resolution" on Sunday, 25th January 1942. As soon as we were safely anchored a tender came alongside with workmen and timber to rebuild the storm damage in the soldiers' accommodation. Bunker fuel, fresh water and stores were taken aboard. The weather was extremely hot and it was great to be back in shorts again after battling our way through a force 8 to 9, and having to heave-to to enable the soldiers' accommodation to be temporarily shored up.

No sooner were we anchored than the native "Bum Boats" arrived. This was a new experience for me. The boats were long dug out canoes of varying lengths and full of all manner of fresh fruit – oranges, bananas, mangoes, coconuts, water melon, peanuts, limes, etc. We used our Duty Free cigarettes to barter for the produce, but you had to be very smart to get the better of the traders. They would throw a strong line aboard with a wicker basket attached, into this would go our cigarettes, or money if we had any, then back it would come with whatever one had bargained for.

We upped anchor and proceeded out to sea at midnight on 26th January. We formed up in our same positions in the convoy and continued to head south down the South African coast. Our next port of call was to be Durban. It was amazing what one found out in this convoy. Two of the soldiers aboard were Royal Corp of Signallers and could read Morse visually and also semaphore. When any orders or instructions were being exchanged they simply borrowed the gunlayer's binoculars and read the messages. This is how we were kept fully informed. At the time, the Morse lamp was sheer magic for me, but years later I had to learn it for my Tickets.

The weather stayed hot all the way. A good standard of watch keeping was kept with our extra gunners and signallers and this gave one a feeling of security because we knew that Donetz had his 'U' Boats scattered all the way down the African coast and the South Atlantic. Then as soon as the Japanese came onto the scene, they had them around the Indian Ocean.

Some days could be very quiet and we would break the monotony from time to time with a 'sing along' – Enoch playing his accordion and one of the soldiers a mouth organ.

We arrived at Durban on 13th February 1942. Apart from doing security watch – to flood the magazine in case of fire – we all got a good run ashore. It was really great to stretch our legs after the long sea voyage from Greenock – 32 days.

Durban looked impressive and we soon discovered they brewed a good quality beer and their brandy was cheap. The troopship that docked at Durban gave all the soldiers shore leave, as did the Royal Navy escort ships – not forgetting crews and gunners of the Merchant Navy cargo ships. The result was that all the main streets of Durban became jammed with servicemen, and as the day wore on the inevitable happened. The servicemen had too much to drink and it caused a headache for the Military Police who had to ferry the men back to their respective ships. This made headlines in most of the newspapers the following day and it reflected badly on us.

We did not know at this time that the Japanese army had penetrated all the way down Malaysia and must have been at the back door to Singapore preparing to cross the narrow channel into that country. Apparently the powers that be could not decide where an invasion might take place but finally decided it would be a sea-borne invasion so all the main defences were placed facing out to sea to repel an invasion. That is why this huge convoy, consisting of thousands of troops and seven cargo ships, scupper deep with equipment, was destined for Singapore. The powers that be were at least three months late in making the decision to send us out there. However, on Sunday, 15th February, two days after we arrived at Durban, it was announced that Singapore had surrendered.

The H.M.S. Prince of Wales and H.M.S. Repulse had both reached Singapore on December 2nd 1941. Admiral Sir Tom Phillips took over command Far Eastern Fleet on December 6th. On December 9th 1941, both ships were sunk. H.M.S. Repulse by 12.30 and H.M.S. Prince of Wales by 13.20. Out of 2,800 men in the two ships crews, 2,000 were saved including Admiral Phillips. 800 brave seamen were killed.

The Japanese conquered Malaysia in fifty four days. Their casualties were about 4600 British casualties about 5,400, but a large part of this figure were taken prisoner and had to face the living hell of the Japanese horror camps.

On Sunday night of February 8th 1942, the invading force crossed the narrow

75

channel separating Singapore from the mainland. The crossing was made on an 8-mile stretch of the 30-mile straits, which at this point was less than 1 mile wide. This section was held by three battalions of the 22nd Australian brigade. The Japanese strength was over 30,000 troops. We had roughly 85,000 troops under the command of General Percival – mainly British, Australian, Indian and some local Malaysian and Chinese Units. The fall of Singapore came on Sunday, February 15th, exactly one week after the Japanese landing. On the evening of Sunday, February 15th 1942, General Percival presumably went out under a white flag to the Japanese Commander, hoping that he would obtain better treatment for his British troops. When one looks at the maps and charts of this area, it is hard to understand the way the Chiefs of Staff had decided to defend Singapore. All their guns facing out to sea to fight off a sea-borne invasion when it seems so obvious that an invasion force would march and capture Malaysia, then cross the narrow strip of water and in through the back door where there was not even a single gun emplacement. Sixteen troopships and seven cargo ships sent thousands of miles for nothing.

It came as a shock to all of us to hear the sad news of the fall of Singapore. The question was now where do we go from here. We were all waiting for a decision from Whitehall. It was not to come until February 16th.

We sailed round the coast to a small bay (Sultana Bay). We anchored and were on our own. The reason being that we were carrying enormous supplies of ammunition (depth charges and mines). The shipwrights in Newport had constructed a huge wooden box in No.1 hold and whatever was stowed in it was surrounded and packed in sand. The powers that be were making sure that in case of fire we did not blow up any other ship in the vicinity.

Sultana Bay was very calm and it was here that I saw my first penguins in the wild. Enoch again produced some fishing lines. This time it was a success and the fish we caught was Red Gurnard. They had a large head and mailed cheeks and three finger line pectoral rays used to feel their way around the seabed. The largest ones were cut up and handed over to the cook. We swung around the anchor for days, but it was not all fishing and swimming. The Master gave the order not to swim because of sharks.

The strong sunshine gave us all a good sun tan but to prevent sunburn we boiled used tea leaves, let it get cold and rubbed this over our arms and shoulders. Coconut oil was cheap and gave a quicker tan than did tea.

We took the opportunity while here to paint the 4" gun and the gun deck and the shell holders, etc. The machine-guns were removed from their mountings, carried along to No.5 hatch, stripped one by one, cleaned and oiled and reassembled.

On February 20th we sailed back to Durban, took on water and stores and bunkers. The Master had received his sailing orders and we were to join Convoy D.M.3 on February 22nd. The Convoy consisted of the following ships: "Aagtekerk", "Autolycus", "Christiaan Huygens", H.M.S "Colombia", "Empire Woodlark", "Pardo", "Port Chalmers", "Staffordshire" and "Strathnaver". The battleship, H.M.S. Ramillies, and the destroyer, Norman, escorted the Convoy. Following the surrender of Singapore, the orders for the convoy were changed and we were to proceed to Batavia. These orders were altered again in consequence of the Japanese advance and the convoy was diverted to Colombo. Following yet another change of orders, the Merchant Cruiser "Corfu" (which had joined on 29th February), along with "Aagtekerk", "Christiaan Huygens", "Empire Woodlark", "Port Chalmers" and "Strathnaver", detached from the convoy on 2nd March and proceeded to Bombay. The remaining vessels, including "Pardo", arrived at Colombo on 4th March.

Note – See ADM/199/1211 dated 7th March 1942. Convoy was A & B and D.M.3 was also split into A & B portions. In consequence of the fast advance of the Japanese army, instead of proceeding to Batavia it was split and some were re-routed to Bombay and some to Colombo.

W.S.15 split into W.S.15 A & B and D.M.3 on 22nd February.

D.M.3 split into A & B portions on 2nd March.

4th March 1942. We arrived safely in Colombo in the early hours of the morning and secured fore and aft to the bouys facing out to sea. The harbour was full of ships. The battleship Ramillies, cruisers Dorsetshire and Cornwall, destroyer Tenedos, and the Blue Funnel A.M.C. Hector, a Dutch destroyer whose name I cannot recall, and a South African minesweeper H.M.S.A. Springbok.

Later on the soldiers on board were disembarked via a launch. The ship's lifeboat, equipped with an engine, was lowered ready to take the Master ashore for orders. We wondered what would happen to our cargo as we knew what was down all five holds – a disaster waiting to be ignited.

We had a brief insight as to how far the Japanese army had penetrated since the fall of Singapore. We could read between the lines that they would continue their aggression all the way across the Bay of Bengal, target India and Ceylon for an air base.

The Ship's Purser informed us that we could have an advance on our wages. I wanted some rupees to send some Ceylon tea home. However, we had to wait longer than expected. The Purser went ashore and arrived back to say that he had drawn all the money from the Agent for the whole crew. He removed it from his briefcase, put it on his office desk and locked the door. He then went off to the saloon to have his dinner - overlooking the fact that he had not clamped down the porthole!

After our mid-day meal the Purser sent word along for us to draw our rupees. He let himself into his office, only to discover that the money had vanished. There was pandemonium amidships. The Purser plucked up courage to inform Captain Jones of the robbery. We were told that the total figure stolen was just over £2,000 sterling. At this stage the only people who had boarded us were the Customs to seal the bonded store-room, also a Lt. Commander, D.E.M.S., and an Army Officer to check over armaments. The police were soon aboard and asked question but they realised we were all at our mid-day meal. The stolen money was never found - £2,000 would go a long way in 1942!

After all the excitement we had to wait another day to get our advance. This time the money was brought aboard by the Agent, accompanied by a policeman who stayed in the Purser's office while it was handed out and signed for.

We were sent to yet another safe anchorage because of our highly explosive cargo. It was to be Trincomalee, once again swinging round the anchor all on our own.

At Trincomalee we were once again on our own, as we had been at Sultana Bay because of our cargo of high explosives. The anchorage was shark free so swimming was allowed. This was appreciated by everyone and 'Jacob's ladders' were slung over the bulwarks the whole time.

The only danger was the jellyfish that one encountered. They gave a very painful sting – which I found to my cost! We would swim out to the sand bars a few hundred yards from the anchorage where there was white coral and an abundance of beautiful coloured tropical fish.

We still carried out our gun drills, of course, and the armaments were cleaned and ready for action. One of the sailors said that while he was working in the wheel house he had overheard the Master say that it was assumed by the 'Top Brass' that the island would be subjected to an air attack (not carrier born) to test the Island's defence system, the state of which we did not know. We stayed at our anchorage for three weeks, then we upped anchor and sailed back to Colombo. Once again we were secured to the bouys fore and aft, bows pointing out to sea because it was the Monsoon season. No one wanted to swim in the harbour here – apart from the jelly-fish and venomous water snakes 3'- 4' long, there was the sewage from the ships.

I managed to get ashore to send some tea home. This was quite an experience – it seemed to be a world of professional beggars. There were children who I was told had been crippled by their parents so they could beg for them. They would all use the same chant "Sa'ib - no mama, no papa, no mongee (food), one Anna, give me one Anna". (An Anna is just $1/16^{th}$ of a Rupee). It was a pathetic sight to see so many children begging and a sight you don't forget.

Another sad sight was to see many natives with the disease "elephantiasis". I learnt that this was a skin disease due to a nematode parasite that causes gross enlargement of the limb, normally the leg. One poor native carried a placard that stated his leg was 25" round.

The ship's motor boat was kept busy taking the Master to twice-daily conferences. We realised by now the intention of the Japanese who were fully operational and sinking many ships in the Bay of Bengal.

The native gangs of stevedores began discharging our cargo that had been destined for Singapore. We were all curious to know what had been loaded at Cardiff in December 1941. The Boson was instructed to rig fire hoses to all five holds and also sand buckets. The Chief Engineer was told to make sure that the Deck Service was on at all times ready for action in case of fire (the dread of all seamen). I don't fully recall the speed at which the cargo was discharged but it was slower than our dockers in the U.K. would have taken.

There was a selection of Navy ships in the harbour – H.M.S. Cornwall and H.M.S. Dorsetshire on our starboard side and also a Dutch Cruiser. Ahead of us was the South African Corvette H.M.S.A.S. Springbok, and astern of us, undergoing repairs, was H.M.S. Tenedos.

Tied up just inside the entrance to the harbour was the Blue Funnel passenger cargo ship "Hector", now H.M.S. "Hector". The "Hector" was built in 1924, 11,198 GRT, by Scotts Shipbuilding & Engineering Co. Greenock, for the Ocean Steam Ship Company for the cargo and passenger service to Australia. In 1939 she was requisitioned by the Admiralty for us as an armed cruiser and commissioned as H.M.S. Hector. On April 5th 1942 when the Japanese attacked Colombo, she was bombed and set on fire and sank at her moorings. At the time she was being de-commissioned. The loss of life during the attack was thirteen.. The wreck was formally handed back to the Ocean Steam Ship Company on 20th April 1942. It was 1946 when she was raised, broke away from her tow and was beached and then sold for scrap where she lay. A very sad end for such a beautiful old passenger cargo ship.

During the first week of April 1942, I received a letter from home telling me that my cousin, Arthur, was serving aboard H.M.S. Cornwall. He had joined the Royal Navy before the war and was a Chief Petty Officer, Engine Room. He had served on H.M.S. Kelly under Lord Mountbatten's command when he was sunk off Crete. Our Gunnery Officer said he would try and get me aboard H.M.S. Cornwall, and that one of the sailors would take me round on the Sunday. He added, "Put your No.1's on and attend the Church Service".

There was always a lot of activity in the harbour ferrying the various Ships' Masters to and from Naval H.Q. The Naval D.E.M.S. and the Army Maritime Ack-Ack Officers came aboard for armament and accommodation inspection, and this was followed by gun drill.

The Lt. Commander offered a lift to anyone who wanted to go ashore. I took advantage of the offer as I wanted to buy some souvenirs to take home. While on shore I made a visit to the Union Jack Club – which was nice and cool inside. One didn't stay ashore very long – firstly, the heat was really oppressive, secondly one was surrounded and could hardly move for beggars, and thirdly most of the natives chewed 'Betel' and spat it everywhere. This made the streets look pretty revolting. The 'Betel' is the leaf of an evergreen plant called the Piper-Betel that is chewed along with the 'Areca-nut-parings'.

On Saturday, April 4th, the Master came back from H.Q. and all leave was stopped. The machine-guns on the Bridge and boat deck were uncovered and kept in a state of readiness. Likewise the Bofor 40 m.m. manned by the Army gunners (later to prove a disaster for the defence of our ship). Apparently the Japanese had aircraft carriers somewhere in the vicinity. The harbour was more active than ever now as the crews of the Naval ships were rounded up ashore and ferried back to their ships.

Just before midnight, H.M.S. Cornwall and H.M.S. Dorsetshire slipped their moorings and disappeared into the pitch black night and we were never to see them again. I heard from home at a later date that my cousin had survived a second time. As the Navy ships sailed out a single red light was switched on above the jetty, which spelled out that an attack was imminent. We were told that this would probably be at daybreak on Sunday, April 5th. I rolled a few cigarettes and tried to sleep as we knew dawn came early.

I cannot recall exactly what time sunrise was on April 5th 1942, but we were all closed up at our action stations. The Marlin 303 machine-guns on each wing of the Bridge were manned by the two cadets. The two Hotchkiss 303 machine-guns on the boat deck were manned by me on the port side, and another seaman gunner on the starboard side.

The Bofor 40 m.m. mounted abaft of the 4" gun on a raised platform was manned by the Army gunners.

The stars were gradually being snuffed out as daylight crept in from the East and very soon the dawn was upon us. The Master, Chief and Second Officers were on the Bridge making a sweep of the sky with binoculars.

It was the Chief Officer who yelled out and pointed skywards. What we saw were high altitude bombers, but they were far too high for our machine guns. They appeared to be flying in from our port quarter and across the ship to the starboard wing of the Bridge. Someone yelled out "bombs" but I had already seen them fall from the belly of the twin- engine bombers. They quickly got bigger and I remember saying out loud "God, we've had it". However, I thank God I was wrong. A stick of three bombs hit the harbour clear of our starboard bow, the force of the explosion created a huge surge and it literally lifted the bows out of the water. We ranged up and down for what seemed to be an eternity and we thought that some of the moorings would carry away. Luckily, they held fast and she settled down again.

Another wave of bombers came in from our stern and the Army gunners decided to have a go at this wave. However, they only got five rounds away and then the gun jammed; they could not get it firing again try as they might. We had relied on the Bofor 40 m.m. to defend us and our lovely fast cargo ship. It had now let us down. If only we had been armed with a few Oerlikon 20 mm we could have put up a far better defence. The Zero dive bombers followed the twin-engine bombers. They attacked H.M.S. Hector the A.M.C. She had been hit by the first attack and was already on fire when the Zeros singled her out and scored more direct hits. They also attacked H.M.S. Tenedos who was way over on our starboard quarter, tied up alongside a repair wharf. She was hit and set on fire. It was one of the Zero dive bombers that attacked the Tenedos, then banked round to starboard, flew round and came in from our port quarter. He was roughly 'half-mast high', a sitting duck. I fired one full strip into him. I could see the pilot quite plainly. He made it over the breakwater and crashed into the sea. The South African ship moored ahead of us, H.M.S.A.S. Springbok, did not open fire on this single dive bomber, neither did the cadet manning the Marlin 303 on the port wing of the bridge.

We got the order to stand down from the Gunnery Officer. We did think that a tot of rum would be the order of the day, but to our disappointment it was not forthcoming. Most of us trooped along to the Chief Steward and got our allocation of 2 x ½ pint bottles of beer. Ship routine was back to normal, but the guns were manned again just before sunrise.

On the Monday morning at about 10 a.m. the Red Ensign was lowered to half-mast – as were the flags on all the other ships in the harbour. A barge was taking all the sailors who had been killed in action aboard H.M.S. Hector. The barge carrying them passed under our stern. A total of 13 brave sailors laid side by side wrapped in their hammocks was a very sad sight. They were to be buried ashore.

No native labour appeared that morning to carry on with the discharge of our cargo. Apparently, the natives had gone into the hills. It was some days before they appeared again. We were told they were bribed into coming back to work. They were given Navy uniforms and caps and that did the trick!

Our cargo was quickly discharged of every kind of explosive imaginable, from 303 ammunition to 15" shells for the Naval guns facing out to sea at Singapore. Also artillery shells for the Army and depth charges for the Royal Navy. The Chief Officer remarked it was a good thing the stick of bombs had missed us! He thanked me for what I did during the attack and said it had not gone unnoticed.

Before the cargo was discharged, a Royal Naval launch came alongside and the working party had two large tarpaulins hoisted aboard along with crates of stores. As soon as No. 5 hold was discharged, the sailors flattened out the derricks. One of the new tarpaulins was stretched across the hatch over the old one. The second one, which was larger, was dropped over the derricks and made secure. We soon learnt that we were taking more than 100 Royal Navy survivors from H.M.S. Prince of Wales and H.M.S. Repulse to Cape Town.

The following day the survivors came aboard and made themselves at home under the tarpaulin. Regardless of what they had endured after being sunk by the Japanese, they were a happy crowd and they said that at Cape Town they were going to join a troopship bound for the U.K. and "survivor's leave".

One survivor from the "Prince of Wales" who was a pre-war sailor, told us how they had narrowly missed being sunk by the Bismark. One of the Bismark's huge shells penetrated through the "Prince of Wales" armour plate, it lodged near a magazine but did not explode. He went on to say that when they removed it they discovered that it had been sabotaged at the great Skoda armaments factory in Czechoslovakia by means of a layer of hard setting cement being laid under the fuse cap before the nose-cap was inserted. This was lucky for everyone, it was sad enough losing H.M.S. Hood.

The weather stayed good all the way. The cooks were kept busy feeding all the extra sailors but help was given wherever possible.

We went alongside in Cape Town and the sailors were taken ashore. We then took on bunkers, fresh water and stores and were away again. We headed in a South Westerly direction, and after a few days we assumed we would be going to Australia. We were somewhere in the South Atlantic. The weather was deteriorating. The great grey beards of the Southern Ocean rolled on unceasingly and it appeared to be higher than the vessel. The wind worked its way up to gale force and we were shipping huge green seas right over the fo'c's'le head and cascading over the fore deck with ever increasing regularity. The ship rolled, pitched and shuddered as she tried to shake herself from the clutches of these huge waves. It made life very uncomfortable. We were battling through gale force 10 winds It was a scything wind that tried to cut right through you. An unforgettable experience and one I was going to live through again on a later occasion.

On 22nd June 1942 at 08.00 hrs, land was sighted ahead of us. Visibility was poor but we could make out the outline of South Georgia. The Master was on the Bridge and gave the order to bring the ship round to W.N.West. In doing so we were hit on the starboard side by a mountainous sea. Luckily, no one was in the vicinity. The starboard lifeboat was swung out but this huge volume of sea water that slammed into us just literally bent over the radial davit at the after end and left it at a grotesque angle. The after rope falls were unshipped from the davit head and it was left suspended by the for'ard falls only. All the gear was cast into the sea, mast, oars and sails and anything that was loose or moveable.

By 08.13 it was all hands on deck – the Chief Officer and the Bosun were quickly on the scene. The Master stayed on the Bridge with the Third Mate. Speed was reduced and he manoeuvred her into a position where the very hazardous boat rescue operation could be carried out. Captain Jones was an excellent seaman and had undergone the rigours of rounding 'The Horn' in his younger days and had served his time under sail.

A method was quickly worked out whereby we could retrieve the lifeboat, which at every roll of the ship appeared to be in its death throws. No matter how well the ship was manoeuvred to enable the sailors to come to grips with her, a wave would come crashing against us and the lifeboat would veer away into the trough of the sea, or be carried back to slam up against the ship's side on the crest of another wave. It was a miracle as to how the for'ard falls were not ripped out. The mousing had been put on very securely – either by a good rigger or a good seaman – and this pre-vented the hook on the top block jumping out. That is how the after falls came adrift. The power of the sea that struck us just simply smashed it off, allowing the top block to jump out. The only method was to put a bowline in the new 2" rope and get it hooked over the hook that took the bottom block of the falls. After many attempts one of the sailors man-aged to lasso it, and the sailors laid back on the rope and kept it taut while the winchman on No.4 starboard winch took up the slack that had been rove through a single block secured to the head of the bent after-davit via a number of single blocks they had secured on the boat deck and down to the winch-barrel.

It was a very clever rig that had been worked out, and it was vital that they did their utmost to save the lifeboat in case we were torpedoed or blasted out of the water by surface raiders which were operating in the South Atlantic. The Chief Officer said if this happened we could always cut the lashings and hope she would float free as the ship went down! As soon as the sailors raised the lifeboat to above the level of the boat deck, we all lent a hand and it was manhandled on to the boat deck where it was lashed down and secured in chocks. The time was now 09.45. The sailors were all given a tot of rum – but not the gunners who had also helped! Chippy said this was very mean and, much to our satisfaction, produced a bottle of rum for us.

As we headed further north the weather began to improve and the sea no longer came crashing down over the fo'c's'le head. We had ventured down as far as 54 degrees south which was an unforgettable experience for most of us. When the sailors came down from the wheel, they said our course was now north west, but which port were we going to arrive at? We could do 15 knots if the Master deemed it prudent, and we quickly lapped up the mileage. On 30th June 1942 we arrived at Porto Alegre, Rio Grande do Sol, Brazil. The ship was made fast port side to, and at 16.00 hrs. No.1 lifeboat and damaged radial davit were sent ashore to be repaired.

It soon became known why we had come all this way. A full cargo of bully-beef for the Eighth Army in the Middle East. It was good to see the ship lit up again and see the shore lights.

The Master informed Eric that all the ammunition must be stowed away. The 4" B.L., the Bofor 40 m.m. and all the machine-guns to be kept covered and someone on watch at all times. This was in case of saboteurs. According to what we had been told by the D.E.M.S. Officers in the U.K., South America was a favourite operating base for Nazi spies. We wore civilian clothing when we ventured ashore, simply acting the part of Merchant seamen. At least we had the opportunity to catch up on our sleep when we came off watch.

The following day we had a good look round. A large wooden-fenced corral was filled to the limit with cattle. We could not guess what breed they were, they appeared to be of a mixed breed. Some were identified as the famous breed of Herefords. Nearby were two large buildings which were the abattoirs. The meat was processed and then tinned, either small tins or large 7 lb size. The tins were labelled and then moved into the refrigeratorium to cool off and then packed into wooden boxes ready for loading aboard into "Pardo's" five huge holds and tween decks.

I had my 20th birthday between Cape Town and Porto-Alegre and the two Eric's (the Gunlayer and the Chippy) said they would take me for a birthday treat when we made Port. True to their word, the three of us went ashore and I was treated to a huge steak grilled over charcoal. It was over a pound in weight and the taste was superb – with this was served two eggs and a mountain of chips. There was a floor show taking place at the time and there were some very beautiful dancing girls. The leading lady and singer, Carmen, was wearing a glamorous green velvet evening gown and I couldn't help but fall in love with her. She came across to our table and Eric told her we were celebrating my 21st birthday. Eric could speak her language fairly well. I don't know what he told her but this beautiful girl spent the evening sitting alongside me and I gather she wanted me to take her home. Although my ship mates were urging me on I resisted the temptation! This was mainly because I had a girl friend at home. As it happens my girl friend married an American serviceman while I was away at sea. When the sailors found out that I had let such an opportunity pass I received quite a lot of flack and ribald comments from them!

The dockers worked quickly and we gradually got down to our marks. We had a full cargo of bully beef. The lower holds and the tween decks must have held thousands of cases. Before we sailed we had another visit from the D.E.M.S. Officer, who was in 'civvies' as he was in a neutral country, and he gave us the usual pep talk. Bunkers were topped up and the fresh water tanks, and the Chief Steward's stores and fresh vegetables were hoisted aboard. The No.1 lifeboat had been repaired and made seaworthy and the two cadets had put all the rations back into the galvanized containers and filled the water butts. The sailors then hoisted her clear of the chocks and swung her out and into the sea-going position and bowsed in. We cast off after dark and headed out into the South Atlantic, relying on our speed to get us to our destination. We shaped a course into the Indian

Ocean, where Japanese subs were operating and taking a steady toll of Merchant ships. Then round into the Gulf of Aden, into the Red Sea and on to Suez, the southern most end of the canal where our valuable cargo was destined for the Eighth Army and the Royal Air Force. Look-out watches were set again. One Naval gunner on the 4" gun deck and one Maritime gunner in the Bofors raised gun emplacement. The old routine, 4 hours on and 4 hours off. The sailors informed us that they were steering a South-easterly course towards South Africa. Fortunately, we did not encounter the horrific weather conditions we had experienced from South Georgia to Porto-Alegre. We were also down to our marks with a full cargo. "Pardo" behaved extremely well when she was fully loaded. Just a long steady roll and very little sea taken aboard.

The menu aboard ship changed slightly since we sailed from Brazil. For instance, breakfast would now consist of fried bully beef and eggs, and for dinner, the Chef would make a corned beef hash. This made a change from dried cabbage and potato and ships biscuits. On very hot days we had salads with bully beef. The sailors found two unopened cases of small tins under the fo'c's'le head . They assumed it had been put there by the dockers to be taken ashore. One by one the tins found their way aft to the sailors and gunners accommodation, so if a meal was not too good we had our own supply of bully beef.

As we rounded the Cape of Good Hope, we could make out the lights of Cape Town, Port Elizabeth and Durban. The course was then set to take us up through the Mozambique Channel, so we had South Africa on our port side and Madagascar on our starboard. This was a prudent decision by the Master, assuming that the Japanese submarines would not venture so close inshore as there are numerous small islands scattered about to the west and also to the north east of Madagascar.

After the attack on Pearl Harbour on 7th December 1941, it did not take long for the Japanese High Command to order their Submarine Captains to sink anything that came into their sight. They had an extremely large area to carry out their operations. The whole of the Indian Ocean, Bay of Bengal, Straits of Malaysia, the whole of the Australian coastline, across the Tasman to New Zealand, the seas around Indonesia and New Guinea, the South China seas and the Philippines, Hong Kong, Taiwan and the East China seas to Shanghai.

I cannot name all the ships that were sunk up to the time we were bound for Egypt during 1942, but the following is the approximate tonnage

December 10th to December 24th 1941	5,350	gross tons
January 3rd to January 31st 1942	99,401	" "
February 3rd to February 28th 1942	64,920	" "
March 1st to March 22nd 1942	46,924	" "
April 2nd to April 10th 1942	32,885	" "
May 1st to May 30th 1942	43,136	" "
June 5th to June 30th 1942	74,678	" "
July 1st to July 9th 1942	28,818	" "
Total	**396,112**	" "

Note: May's tonnages include H.M.S. Ramillies, the British Loyalty at Diego Suarez.

(Professor Jurgen Rohwer has kindly given me permission to take this extract from his much acclaimed book "Axis Submarine Successes of World War Two").

We crossed the equator for the third time and the weather gradually got warmer. It was good to change into our tropical rig of shorts and gym shoes. We entered the Gulf of Aden and into the Red Sea. This was the first time for me. We arrived at our destination at the southern most end of the canal and made fast to a very old wharf. The derricks had been topped and the tarpaulins stripped off all five holds. The shore gangs lost no time in getting aboard to start discharging our cargo and they worked round the clock. When it got dark the ship was lit up with clusters and all we gunners had to do was continue with our normal fire and security watch. We had the usual visit by the D.E.M.S. and Maritime Officer. This was a war zone and there was nothing to see ashore. All the wharfs and any spaces were piled high with war equipment – tanks, trucks, jeeps, guns, ambulance and fighter planes. Most of our cargo was discharged straight onto army and R.A.F. lorries – there was a never-ending convoy of vehicles.

A good Service canteen sold bottles of Tennants beer and cheap cigarettes. The natives made a strong drinking glass out of the empty pint bottles by simply cutting the neck out at the shoulder and then smoothing it down with a sandstone wheel. Quite a few found their way back on board.

We sailed under cover of darkness as soon as the last case was safely ashore. Back the way we came, crossing the equator for the fourth time down the Mozambique channel, round the Cape of Good Hope and the long haul to Porto-Alegre for yet another full load of bully beef for Egypt. We were blessed once again with a safe voyage, passing the occasional fast ship like ours, relying on their speed and good seamanship to get through. Who knows what was lurking underneath us in that vast expanse of ocean. The only company we had were the giant Albatross that followed us for days waiting for any food to be thrown into the 'Boson's locker'. One good thing they could always rely on was vegetable peelings and trimmings from the galley. These amazing birds stayed in the air for weeks and strange as it may seem they seldom flew north of the equator.

As soon as we arrived at Porto-Alegre the dockers got to work again, loading into all five holds. The Master had to leave us here the day we arrived as he was to be operated on for varicose veins. The Chief Officer was promoted Master during his absence. We sorted out the fire and security watches so we would know how much time we would have ashore. We had no problems getting our full cargo loaded. After a week the Master returned to the ship and after midnight we cast off and headed once again into the South Atlantic Ocean. We were soon back into our routine. There were always plenty of books in the Purser's library and we had a huge collection of American magazines which we enjoyed.

The Cape of Good Hope soon appeared way over on our port side and we crossed the equator for the fifth time. This was getting to be a habit with

"Pardo". The remark was made that we would never get back home in this ship as she was too fond of the tropics! We quickly lapped up the mileage and arrived in port to get the bully beef unloaded as fast as possible. We managed to get over to the canteen to buy some beer and cigarettes. During the evening we got out the mosquito nets to avoid being eaten alive. The D.E.M.S. and Maritime Officers came aboard and we were informed that we would not be going back across the South Atlantic.

When the last sling of cargo was landed on the wharf, the sailors quickly covered the hatches, flattened out the derricks and spread the tarpaulins. We proceeded down the Red Sea and as we cleared the Gulf of Aden the sailors told us they were steering a course of East x North, which would take us over to India. We soon established that we were bound for Bombay. There were many stories from those of the crew who had been to Bombay before.

We arrived there early morning and did not have to wait long for the Pilot to come aboard and get us alongside. Before lunch the D.E.M.S. and Maritime staff came aboard and I was informed that I would be signing off the following day, August 4th 1942. Transport would be alongside at 10.00 hrs. Apparently gunners were required for a troopship and that is where I was headed. I had never served on a large ship and I was keen to get started on the journey. I packed my kit and carefully wrapped the wooden carvings I had bought in Ceylon. I had plenty of room for packing as D.E.M.S. gunners were issued with a second kit-bag. This was to carry our tropical and cold weather gear. I had accumulated quite a lot of luggage during the 11 months and 26 days I had served on this lovely fast and efficient ship. I said my farewells to Captain Jones, the Chief Mate and the rest of the crew. She had been a very happy ship and I was sorry to leave her.

M.V. PARDO   List of Officers, Crew and Gunners

Arthur Jones	Master
Carlton Dingle	Chief Officer
Dennis Warren	Second Officer (and our Gunnery Officer)

Arthur Wilson	Third Officer
Stanley Harris	First Radio Officer
Albert Young	Second Radio Officer
Arthur Steen	Third Radio Officer
Thomas Tron	Chief Engineer
Cecil Ford	Second Engineer
Ernest Hodgson	Third Engineer
Thomas Rawson	Fourth Engineer
Edward Roberts	Junior Engineer
William McArthur	Junior Engineer
Douglas Howard	Junior Engineer
John Dyer	Electrician
Clerk (Dip)	Christopher Cummins
Arthur Hennessey	Chief Steward
Nicholas Cox	Assistant Steward
Ernest Golding	Assistant Steward
Frederick Archer	Assistant Steward
Hugh Williams	Stewards Boy
Andrew McCorick	Stewards Boy
Robert Jones	Chief Ships Cook
Joseph Stringfellow	Second Cook and Baker
Ernest Rich	Galley Boy
Eric Rankin	Carpenter
John Jackson	Boatswain
Samuel Lines	Lamptrimmer A/B
Ernest Mockford	A/B (Deserted ship – 3.5.42.)
Sidney Bicker	A/B
William Bell	A/B
William Cook	A/B
Robert Mooney	A/B
Arthur Smith	A/B
Evanangelos Athans	A/B
Leonard Holdgate	Sailor

Curfyl Lewis	Sailor
George Coster	Ordinary Seaman
William Williams	Ordinary Seaman
William McQuillan	Engine Room Storekeeper
Charles Thompson	Diesel Greaser Cleaner
John Walsh	Diesel Greaser Cleaner
James Lloyd	Diesel Greaser Cleaner
Albert Mitchell	Cleaner (Deserted ship – 22.12.41.)
Samuel Rogers	Cleaner (Deserted ship – 22.12.41.)
Hugh Patterson	Cleaner (Deserted ship – 22.12.41.)

D.E.M.S. Gunners

Eric Roberts	Gunlayer
William Townend	Seaman Gunner (Signed off after our first voyage to South America)
George Grassick	Seaman Gunner
John Withell	Seaman Gunner (Signed on at Liverpool for voyage to Singapore)

Maritime Ack-Ack Gunners

Jack Saltmore	Bofors Gun Crew – Corporal I/C
William Ball	Bofors Gun Crew
Wilstone Be Harrell	Bofors Gun Crew
Percy Morris	Bofors Gun Crew
George Smith	Bofors Gun Crew
John Dickens	Bofors Gun Crew
Lachlan Glendinning	Second Lieutenant. Signed on at Gourock

along with fourteen soldiers to take passage to Singapore. They had to disembark at Ceylon because of the fall of Singapore.

S.S. YOMA

Chapter 6

FROM M.V. "PARDO" TO D.E.M.S. BARRACKS, BOMBAY, AND S.S. "YOMA"

It took us about half an hour to arrive at the D.E.M.S. Barracks in Bombay. After reporting in, documentation, etc., I was shown the accommodation. It was a large, well- ventilated brick hut accommodating about twenty personnel. Ten beds down each side of the hut and all the beds had mosquito nets rigged over them. There was a decent sized mess-deck five minutes walk away.

The Commandant was Captain Bell, a veteran of World War I. He was too old for active service but was doing a vital job of being O.C. of this large barracks. He made a point of interviewing everyone and I met him the day after I arrived. The meeting lasted 15 minutes - it was very informal, and he asked a lot of questions about the Japanese air attack on Ceylon.

After the meeting I discovered I had no duties, so decided to do some sightseeing. After getting the 'all clear' from the Duty Officer I went outside the barracks and hailed a rickshaw to take me into the City of Bombay. It seemed very much like Ceylon but a lot busier. Crowds jostling the footpaths and betel nut being spat in every direction. There were far more beggars than I had encountered in Ceylon.

There were a few cinemas in the City, but the air conditioning never worked very well. However, one could get plenty of cold drinks to cool down. The biggest gamble when going to the cinema was to get bitten by bugs! The seats in the cinemas were made of cane and platted string, and the seats were infested with these insects.

On one occasion I was asked to go out to a firing range to test fire the Oerlikon 20 m.m. anti-aircraft gun. How I wished that we could have had these on M.V. "Pardo" when we were fighting off the zero dive-bombers. We also tested the new 4" dual purpose submarine and anti-aircraft gun. Fixed charge in the brass container. There was no loading in the cordite charge and it was much quicker to load and fire.

While in Bombay I managed to get included in a soccer team for a couple of matches and this certainly broke the monotony.

I had seven days to wait before I was posted to my third ship. I was told on the 11th that I would be joining a ship called the S.S. "Yoma" on 12th August. I therefore reported to the M.O. for a medical examination.

After breakfast on 12th August the R.N. Transport took me to the docks to join S.S. "Yoma" which was a troop ship. She was built by Wm. Denny Bros. Of Dunbarton for Paddy Henderson Shipping Company. Her gross tonnage was 8,131 and Port of Registry Glasgow. Off/Number 80289.

Armament 1 x 4" B.L. Mk. 1 x

1 x 12 Pdr. 12 cwt. HA/LA. Mk 2A

4 x Oerlikons 20 m.m.

D.E.M.S. Gunners 9, Army Gunners 6.

I got acquainted with the other gunners and was shown where all our defences were situated. I stayed aboard that evening, but my stay was going to be short lived. The following day, 13th August, an explosion occurred in the engine room resulting in some casualties. Two ambulances came to the ship and five of the engine room crew were whisked away. I was told two of the firemen died on their way to hospital. It was not divulged at the time what had caused the explosion or the nature of the casualties.

The Gunnery Officer came along and informed me and four other D.E.M.S. gunners that we would be collected at 10 a.m. on the 14th, so it was back to barracks to wait for a posting to my next ship.

From Lloyds Register of Shipping and Kew Records Office, I have obtained the relevant information regarding the sinking of S.S. "Yoma". Lloyds War Losses records the sinking date of 17th June 1943. "Yoma" was on a course from Sfax Tripolitania to Alexandria transporting troops. There were 1,845 personnel on board, including 160 crew members, 15 gunners and 1,670 troops. Of this number, 30 crew members, 3 gunners and 451 troops were lost.

Lloyds of London record the position of her sinking as 33 degrees 3'N, 22 degrees 4'East, also that she sank in 500 fathoms.

This is confirmed in Jurgen Rohwer's book "Axis Submarine Successes of World War II 1939-1945", and gives the name of the Commander, the time and position where she was torpedoed.

The S.S. "Yoma" left Sfax Tripolitania on 16th June 1943 in convoy G.T.X2 bound for Alexandria, consisting of five columns of three ships each. Columns to be 4 cables apart. Ships in column to be 3 cables apart. S.S. "Yoma" was convoy number 31.

The following is an extract from Jurgen Rohwer's report.

Date: 17.6.1943

Time: 07.37

Number of submarine: U.81

Commander: Krieg

Position of attack German grid ref: C.O. 5498.

Latitude and longitude: 33 degrees 03'N, 22 degrees 04'East

Note: The S.S. "Yoma" was carrying a large draft of French Naval

personnel from North Africa to reinforce Force "X" at Alexandria.

See the Track chart from H.M.S. Hurworth and the convoy course and approximate time of sinking.

The following is a report by the Chief Officer, Mr. A. Olding:

We were bound from Tripoli to Alexandria, loaded with troops and equipment. The ship was armed with 1 – 4", 1 – 12 pdr., 4 Oerlikons, 4 Hotchkiss, 2 Pillar Boxes and 2 P.A.C. Rockets. The crew, including 9 Navy and 6 Army Gunners, numbered 175, and we carried 134 British Military Officers, 994 British Military Troops, 22 Free French Officers and 643 Free French Naval Ratings as passengers: of this total 30 crew are missing, including the Master, one Writer, 2nd and 3rd Wireless Officers, Chief, 2nd, 4th and 5th Engineers, and 22 crew; I do not know the exact number of casualties amongst the Troops, but approximately 451 of them are missing, in addition 2 R.A.M.C. Orderlies were lost. Only three-quarters of the Free French Officers were saved. Many were injured. All Confidential Books, including the Wireless Codes, were thrown overboard in two weighted boxes. Degaussing was on.

2. We left Tripoli on the 16th June in Convoy G.T.X.2, which consisted of 14 ships, including 3 Troop ships and 3 or 4 L.S.Ts. The convoy was formed in 4 columns, our position being No. 31, the leading ship of the 3rd column, with 2 ships astern. This convoy had a very strong escort. No warnings of submarines being in the vicinity were received, and the convoy proceeded without incident until the 17th June, 1943, when at 17.30, in position 33 degrees 03' N. – 22 degrees 02' E., steering East (approx.), at 6½ knots, we were struck by one torpedo from a U-boat. The weather was fine, sunny with good visibility; there was a calm sea and moderate swell, with light airs, force 2.

3. No one saw the track of the torpedo which struck between the engine room and No. 5 hold on the port side. The "after" engine room bulkhead collapsed, consequently the boiler room, engine room and No. 5 hold flooded immediately. Although the explosion was loud, it was not as loud as I would have expected. The vessel was 'lifted' by the explosion, and settled rapidly by the stern.

4. I was in the Wireless Room at the time. I came out onto the Bridge, but

97

could see nothing owing to the steam which enveloped the ship. The whistle
was blown off the funnel and steam was coming from the whistle steampipe and
from the engine room. Nos. 3 and 4 hatches were blown away, and clouds of
coal dust were thrown high into the air, smothering everything, including myself.
I heard the Master order "abandon ship", and hurried to my lifeboat, which was
No. 6. It was my intention to lower the lifeboats first and then let the men climb
down the ladders into them. None of the crew (Natives), however, turned up
at their boat stations, consequently the troops took it upon themselves to lower
the boats. The native crew lowered and filled the two poop boats without
orders, and altogether six boats were lowered, but at least two were capsized
by the soldiers overcrowding them. I instructed one soldier to help me lower
my lifeboat, and carefully showed him how to do it. Suddenly he let go the
after fall, and the boat went with a run and capsized. I learned later that the
same sort of thing had happened to the 3rd Officer's boat. Lifeboat drill was
practised every day, everybody should have known what to do and all troops
and crew should have gone to their correct lifeboat stations within 3-4 minutes;
there was no excuse for the panic which occurred. By this time the YOMA
was well down by the stern, and the next thing I knew she sank under my feet
and I found myself in the water. The ship carried many rafts, all of which
floated off as the ship went down. Actually there were sufficient boats and
rafts for 2,200 people.

5. I think many of the missing men were trapped in their accommodation when
the ladders from Number 2 messdeck collapsed. As the bow rose into the air
I saw a lot of men on the foc'sle head; they would not jump into the water,
consequently as the bow lifted a number of them lost their footing and fell onto
the bridge, many others being dragged under with the ship. Most of the Free
French personnel did not make any attempt to get into the lifeboats, but imme-
diately jumped overboard. Everybody was wearing a lifebelt.

6. After being a short while in the water two Motor Minesweepers and a British
India ship, which was detailed as Rescue Ship, commenced picking up the
survivors. The British India ship picked up about 160 survivors. I was even-
tually taken on board Minesweeper No. 105, which altogether picked up about
483 men from the water. These minesweepers, which were not part of the

convoy, were bound for Alexandria, and just tagged on to our convoy which happened to be going that way. We were taken to Derna, arriving there at 20.00 the same day. No depth charge attack was made by the escort, I think this was because of the number of men in the water.

7. The European crew and troops behaved fairly well throughout, but I would particularly like to mention the following men:

R.A.M.C. Staff Sergeant Cook, and 4th Officer William Muir

R.A.M.C. Staff Sergeant Cook

Immediately after the explosion Staff Sergeant Cook went to the ship's hospital and got out the three patients, who were suffering from malaria, and put them over the ship's side. He then jumped overboard and hung on to all three men until they were finally rescued by a Minesweeper, about an hour later. They were all wearing lifejackets. He stayed with and attended to them whilst on board the rescue vessel, and on arrival at Derna he accompanied them to the Hospital. His devotion to duty was most outstanding and in the highest tradition of the Medical Service.

4th Officer William Muir

Whilst in the water 4th Officer Muir observed Senior Medical Officer David Cathie, who was stunned and in a semi-conscious condition. Muir went to his assistance, supported him, and towed him for about half an hour toward the Minesweeper, which subsequently picked them up.

8. I consider that all Troopships should be equipped with Carley floats instead of lifeboats, provided they are in escorted convoys where the chances of picking up survivors are good.

The Sinking of S.S. "YOMA"

Approximate number of survivors picked up

H.M.A.S. Gawler	200
H.M.A.S. Lismore	390
Fort Maurepas	40
Motor Minesweeper 102	400

99

Motor Minesweeper 105   350
                            1,380

Survivors were taken to Derna and were landed at 20.00 hrs the same day.
On the Merchant Navy Memorial Tower Hill, only eight names appear:

Paterson, G Master
Bell, H.A.
Cadwell, D.M
Cox, T.R.
Critchell, H.E.
Devlin, R.H.
Guy, W.
Le May, D.E.McG

COURSE INSTRUCTIONS AND ORDERS FOR EVASIVE ACTION FOR A NORTH ATLANTIC CONVOY

Example: SC.122 5-23 March 1943

- 1st Course Instructions of 28 February and 5 March with reference points and stragglers' route.
- 1st order for evasive action.
- 2nd order for evasive action.
- 3rd order for evasive action.
- Actual course.
- Air cover.
- U-boat warning area.
- CHOP-Line.

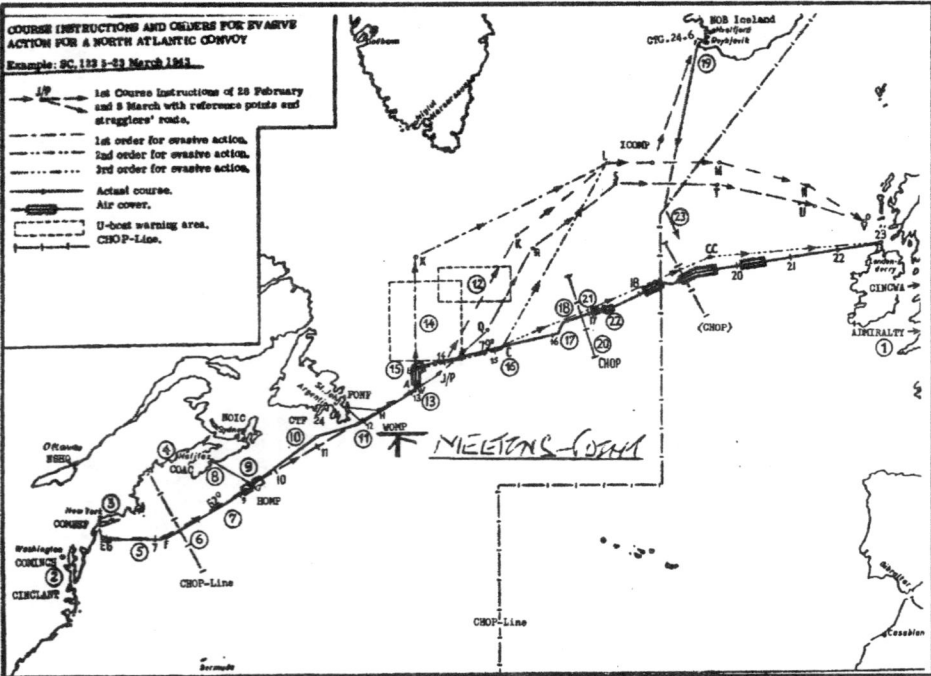

NOB Iceland
CTG.24.6

ICOMP

CTG.24.6

CINCWA

AIRMIRALTY

CHOP

CHOP

MEETING-COMM

FONF

NOIC
CTF 24

Ottawa
NSHQ

COAC

Halifax

New York
COMEF

Washington
COMINCH

CINCLANT

EB

CHOP-Line

Bermuda

CHOP-Line

Casablanca

M.V.NEDERLAND   Dutch Tanker Gross 8,223 Tonns

Built at Wilton Feyenoord Shipyard in Schiedam Near Rotterdam in 1937 After the war she became the "Caltex Nederland" and finally to the breakers yard on the advent of super tankers.

Chapter 7

M.V. NEDERLAND
DUTCH TANKER

Gross Tonnage: 8,223
Port of Registry: The Hague
Official Number: 69,228
Built in Holland: 1937

M.V. Nederland was built at the shipyard of Wilton Feyenoord in Schiedam (near Rotterdam) in 1937. She was registered at Lloyd's Register of Shipping 1942/43. The owner was "Nederlandsche Pacific Tankvaart Maatyschappij".

This information was provided by the Dutch Maritime Museum.

After signing off the S.S. YOMA, I was once again posted back to D.E.M.S. Barracks, Bombay, to await a berth on my fourth ship. This time I was given patrol duties around the perimeter fence. I do not remember how far one had to walk but I do remember it was for two hours. There was always a Duty Officer about and he would come around at any time to check that we were doing our job properly!

I spent a total of 38 days in the Barracks, which seemed a very long time. I occasionally took a rickshaw into Bombay to visit one or other of the Service Canteens for a game of tombola or to enjoy a game of soccer. During this time Vera Lynn flew into Bombay to entertain the troops. Her stage was set in the centre of a large soccer field and there was a huge audience. Everyone enjoyed her visit and it was a terrific morale booster. It's a memory impossible to erase.

It was September before my name appeared on the Posting Board outside Captain Bell's office. I had my medical and discovered that another seaman gunner (William Boldy) was also being posted to the same ship. Naval transport took us both to sign on M.V. Nederland on 21st September 1942. We got our gear aboard, assisted by some of the Chinese crew. Our accommodation was surprisingly spacious and it was large enough for four. The ship was built to carry four passengers and was intended for trading amongst the Dutch East Indies. There was the luxury of electric fans and a good sized wash room and shower.

The accommodation was near to the gun deck which had been built up from the deck below to give more height. The gunner in charge was a Royal Marine Corporal who had served his time and volunteered again after the outbreak of war. He had the rank of Gunlayer.

The Dutch Second Mate came along to introduce himself. He was our Gunnery Officer and spoke very good English. He was a happy and good natured officer. He took us along to the ship's saloon to sign on Ship's Articles. The Master, Captain Hendricus Kopp, was there and he said to us "Look after my ship – we rely on you gunners". The Deck and Engine Room Officers were all Dutch. The sailors, firemen, stewards and cooks were Chinese.

The Gunlayer showed us where the armaments were situated. We had a 4" B.L. tripod mounting on the poop. The deck head of our accommodation had been strengthened to have a 12 pounder mounted - our means of defence against air attacks, along with two 3.03 machine guns, mounted one on each wing of the bridge. Also smoke floats on the gun deck, situated clear of the shell racks.

As soon as our cargo was discharged we set sail for Bahrain Island in the Persian Gulf. As soon as we dropped the pilot, action stations were sounded and the Second Mate put us through our gun drill. Charlie, Bill and myself were assisted by the Chinese crew members who had been put through a gunnery course. They were very efficient. The Chief Mate was in charge of the fire fighting team. When the gun drill was over we set watches.

We found that the Marine Gunlayer had decided to always do the eight to twelve (midnight watch) so that he could get a full night's sleep! I took the twelve to four and Bill the four to eight, but we agreed to change at every port. I preferred the four to eight watch to see the dawn breaking. I was able to observe many really magnificent sunrises. All the time I served on this beautiful ship we never experienced any bad weather. Sometimes the sea was dead calm and occasionally a long low swell that produced a steady roll, accompanied by a graceful rise and fall of her bow and stern.

As we made our way up the Persian Gulf it soon became very hot indeed. I remembered what I had been told by Tanker men with whom I had been shipmates. "When in the Persian Gulf you could fry an egg on the deck!" I was told that tankers used to be called "the trollop of the seas". To take a liking to a tanker is an acquired taste. One may get to like them in a cold platonic way. Probably an entirely different breed of seamen. No heavy cargo gear. No jumbo or heavy lifting gear. No battening down of hatches and spreading tarpaulins, and no cleaning out filthy holds and stacking dunnage.

We were kept on regular voyages between Bahrain Island and South Africa. One trip to Cape Town, then one to Durban. It was always the same cargo. "Aviation fuel" for the Royal Air Force. The Government had inaugurated an air-training scheme somewhere in South Africa and it was our duty to see that they never went short of fuel. The only drawback was that we never had very long alongside. I do not recall the rate fuel was pumped out, but it was normal practice to have just one night in port. The weather was always terribly hot and I do not remember any rainfall all the time we were engaged in that particular run. I soon discovered that a few hours spent ashore was long enough because of the heat.

On one occasion we took an American Engineer from Durban to Bahrain as we had a spare berth in our accommodation. We found him an interesting companion and he gave us a lot of information about America. He also kindly gave us a bottle of whiskey to be shared between the three of us.

On another occasion when we were in Bahrain a fire broke out under the forecastle head. Apparently the Second Mate had forgotten to switch off the degaussing gear and it was about mid-day and very hot. To make matters worse one of the for'ard tanks was overflowing. Aviation fuel was simply pouring on to the fore deck and running into the scuppers and the sea. The fire alarm was sounded and we all charged into action with sand buckets and with whatever fire extinguishers were to hand. Luckily, the fire was quickly extinguished. There was a lot of smoke but the fire did not have a chance to take hold. The Second Mate reacted quickly and got the pumping stopped in the for'ard starboard tank.

One major distraction was that four of the Chinese Engine Room Greasers and Wipers decided to jump overboard to avoid the fire and into the barracuda infested waters where we were berthed. Fortunately, they did not have far to swim to get to another set of wood pylons supporting a second jetty adjacent to us. They clambered up and onto the lower staging, but they found it was impossible to climb up the long pylons and gain access to the road. Seeing their plight, and also the funny side of it, the Chief Mate ordered the motor boat to be lowered to get them aboard. They were lucky the barracudas had not attacked them. The Chinese seamen were first class and they were soon back on board, but they did suffer a lot of sarcastic comments from the sailors.

We cast off after mid-day and as soon as we got clear the Second Mate told us to go along to the Master's cabin. The Master thanked us for helping to get the fire under control and gave us all two bottles of beer. This was really welcome as we could not buy beer aboard the ship.

When we were fully loaded and heading for Cape Town or Durban and the weather freshened up, we got a fair number of flying fish landing on both the fore deck and after deck. They were of varying sizes but they all found their way to the Chinese cook who served up some really good appetizing meals. He gave us some for breakfast and they tasted extremely good, similar to herrings.

We gunners were very fortunate on this ship because we did not have our own mess room and had our meals in the ship's saloon – although not at the same time as the Master and Officers. It was quite a luxury to sit down and have our food served to us by a steward in this beautiful teak and mahogany saloon.

Time passed quickly. After the fire, even though the degaussing gear was working, the Second Mate told us that before we sailed the Royal Navy would have to cut a section out and splice another section in. It did not alter our schedule. They came aboard as soon as we docked and under the supervision of a Lt. Commander, R.N., it only took his team a little over four hours to repair the damage.

I remember Captain Kopp telling us, and this was just after the episode of the fire, that his was a lucky ship. At one time the German Pocket Battleship

Graff-Spee had been laying in wait for the "Nederland" to take her and her full cargo of aviation spirit as a war prize. However, along came the "Africa Shell" "Captain Dove" and, as we all know, the Sparky managed to get a message away which led to the Graff-Spee being driven into Montevideo harbour and finally being scuttled on Hitler's orders.

We had our Christmas aboard "Nederland" in 1942 and we managed to celebrate the occasion with a good Christmas dinner. Both pork and turkey were served and a bottle of beer was placed in front of each table setting. We still kept to our routine of watch keeping but we all thoroughly enjoyed the day.

We arrived in Cape Town on 1st January 1943, and as soon as we were made fast a D.E.M.S. Officer came aboard and informed both Bill and myself that we were to be taken off at noon. We would be staying one night in the Royal Naval barracks at Simonstown and would be signing on a ship that would take us back to England. It was good news as I had not been home since Christmas 1941, and Bill was last home in February 1942. He had a 7-year old daughter in Bradford and he was really pleased to hear he was to be going home. The D.E.M.S. Officer told us that the reason we were going home was the fact that the Navy had a large pool of D.E.M.S. gunners in various ports around the UK, and anyone who had served away from home for more than a year was on the rosta for a UK bound ship.

We quickly got our packing done and said our farewells to the Chief Steward, Mr. Chang. Then along to say goodbye to Captain Kopp and his Officers. Captain Kopp remarked that regretfully he had not seen his own country, Holland, since the summer of 1939.

The Royal Naval transport took us to Simonstown and we arrived at H.M. Naval base at 14.00 hrs.

The "Nederland" survived the war but she became the "Caltex Nederland". She was a beautiful and well kept ship and I particularly remember how well the sailors were looked after. She finally went to the breakers yard although I do not have the year.

From the time I signed off M.V. Pardo in August 1942 to the time I left M.V. Nederland in January 1943, the following tonnages were sunk by both Japanese and German submarines operating in the Indian Ocean and the South African theatre of war:

August 1942	5,237	gross tons
September 1942	28,852	" "
October 1942	188,144	" "
November 1942	169,569	" "
December 1942	23,692	" "

Total tonnage: **415,494**

These figures were taken from Jurgen Rohwer's book "Axis Submarine Successes of World War Two".

U.S.S. Destroyer Greer, escorting convoy S.C.121 along with U.S. Costguard Cutter Spencer. All the way from W.O.M.P.'s to the point where the English escorts come out a couple of days before we made Oversay

U.S. Coastguard Cutter Spencer. Captain Heineman took over all the escorts for Convoy S.C. 121 when we assembled at W.O.M.P.'s February 1943. He also took aboard a large numbr of seamen who had been torpedoed. His actions were superlative at all times. I hope he survived the war.

110

M.V.Gascony. 4,716 Tons Port of Registry, Liverpool Off/Number 60056. Built by A. McMillan at Dumbarton in 1925 for the MacIver Fleet. Her three sister ships being the Lombardy, Saxony and Brittany. In 1932 she was transferred to the Royal Mail Lines. She survived the war. In 1958 she was sold and went to the breakers.

Chapter 8

M.V. GASCONY

After spending just one night at H.M. Naval Barracks, Simonstown, Bill and myself were on the move again. After breakfast we were transported back into Capetown and a launch took us out to join M.V. Gascony. Our new shipmates gave us a hand to get our gear up the gangway and along aft to our accommodation, which was below decks. It was much the same as on M.V. Pardo. The after-end of the tween decks of No.5 hold had been utilised to build accommodation to house six gunners, with a decent sized table in the centre. There was one shower and one toilet. The two gunners who had signed off were grumbling that they had been away from the UK for six weeks, so when we told them we had been away for a year they suddenly went quiet. We had a three-badge Petty Officer in charge, a Scot by the name of Andrews. He was well liked and had a good sense of humour. Quite different from the Marine Corporal we had just left! After dinner we were taken along to the Master's cabin and signed on the Ship's Articles for our sixpence per day! The Master was Captain H.G. Whittle, a Liverpudlian. He was short and stocky and proved to be a very efficient Master – as my story will unfold.

M.V. Gascony was 4,716 gross tons. Port of Registry Liverpool. Official number 60,056. Built by A. McMillan at Dumbarton in 1925 for the MacIver Fleet. Her three sister ships being the Lombardy, Saxony and Brittany. In 1932 she was transferred to the Royal Mail Lines. She survived the war. In 1958 she was sold and went to the breakers yard.

Our ship was waiting for one of the Engineers to come aboard, and as soon as he arrived it was up anchor and away. We quickly got acquainted with the other gunners. Two seaman gunners, both from London (Wilkie and Stokoe), were the best of mates. There was a lot of cockney wit, and there was always a laugh and a joke. The two army gunners were rather different, one was rather scruffy and had little to say, and the other one would burst out in fits of laughter at the least provocation. Wilkie said he was a "nutter" and should never be allowed to handle a machine gun!

As soon as we got underway watches were set, 4 hours on and 8 hours off. The arrangement was two on watch, one on the gun deck where the 4" gun was mounted, and one in the 12 pounder ack-ack gun-pit which was raised and to the rear of the 4" gun.

We discovered that our cargo of Manganese ore was destined for Liverpool. I said excellent, as Liverpool was ideal for me for a train home. I also liked Liverpudlians after experiencing three weeks of continual bombing with them during the great blitz of May 1941.

We were not a fast ship but the powers that be sent us out alone into the vast expanse of the South Atlantic ocean, so we were to take yet another gamble against both surface raiders and submarines. Good weather prevailed and we encountered a very long, low lazy swell and had to adjust our footing to it. The large tonnage of Manganese ore that was in every hold made Gascony develop a regular steady roll. The Bosun remarked "She is going to roll her b .... guts out all the way to Liverpool".

The general topic of conversation now was which port in South America were we heading for to top up in the tween decks. The sailors had been steering a S. Westerly course. The Bosun then told us our destination - we were going to Bahia-Bianca, Argentina, to top up with bully beef, and we were to make sure the cargo gear would be ready. I got out my somewhat battered world atlas and we quickly found where we were bound. Position 38 degrees 35'South. 62 degrees 13'West. I said "thank God", as I recalled the passage I had made in M.V. Pardo to within a few miles of South Georgia in 1942. 54 degrees 30'South. 37 degrees 00 West, and it was very uncomfortable.

After we passed Tristan Da Cunha during the Second Mate's watch at about 14.00 hours, the Look-out on the Forecastle Head spotted what he thought was a periscope fine off the port bow. Quite an easy decision to arrive at as the mast had been left stepped and secured to the thwarts. It was a big mast for the size of the lifeboat and to all intents and purposes the gun crew thought likewise. The Second Mate immediately rang 'Action Stations'. The 4" gun

113

was quickly manned and waiting for the order to load. I was No.2 and the Master had taken over from the Second Mate who was the Gunnery Officer. Between them the Master and the Chief Officer decided that it was a water-logged ship's lifeboat but he must make sure that there were no survivors left in it. The Bosun was ordered to get a derrick topped at No.5 hatch and get it slung aboard. This was speedily carried out and the lifeboat was landed on deck on the starboard side. One of the sailors pulled the plug to drain the seawater out. We discovered that it was No. 17A lifeboat from the Troopship "Orcades".

We resumed our course to Argentina. When the lifeboat had drained the Chief Mate sent the sailors to look around. The only thing to be found was three pairs of large binoculars in their cases. The galvanized tanks were emptied of their contents, which included condensed milk, Horlick tablets, Pemmican and ship's biscuits. These were shared out among the Officers, crew and gunners. It was good to get the condensed milk as our ration was one tin to last us for 10 days. The ship's biscuits were broken up and we mixed them in our soup, and the Pemmican came in very useful when we experienced some cold weather conditions later on. The M.V. "Orcades", to which No.17A lifeboat belonged, was one of P and O's pre-war passenger liners. She was converted to a troopship at the outbreak of war. When she was torpedoed she was homeward bound from South Africa. She was 23,456 gross registered tons and could carry 4,624 troops. She was torpedoed at 10.28 hours on 10th October 1942 by a German submarine, U.172 (Captain Carl Emmerson), in position 31 degrees 51' South. 18 degrees 30' East.

Lifeboat 17A had the whole of the South Atlantic to roam about in from 10th October when she entered the water, until the time we rescued her after passing Tristan Da Cunha. After drifting for over three months she had travelled a long way in a South-Westerly direction. She could have beached herself on the Falkland Islands or the Southern most tip of South America – but we shall never know.

We finally arrived at Bahia on the afternoon of 16th January. We made fast port side to and the dockers came aboard and loading commenced at all five hatches - the tween decks only as all the lower holds held manganese ore that had been loaded at Madagascar before I signed on. It was just a matter of filling up as much of the tween-deck space as possible with cases of corned beef.

We went ashore for a short visit, changing into our civilian clothes as Bahia is part of Argentina. We had been told that anyone found drunk or misbehaving was quickly thrown into the local 'calaboose'. By all accounts, one form of punishment was mucking out the stables before being sent back to our ship. Having only been on this ship since 2nd January, I had very little money to spend, but I was able to buy some nylon stockings to take home as presents. We were back on board fairly early but it was impossible to sleep until the dockers had gone ashore.

They were back aboard for an 8 a.m. start. As soon as one tween deck space was filled up to the deck head, a gang of shore-carpenters were shoring up under the watchful eyes of the Chief Mate. It had to be secure for the North Atlantic, which everyone assumed would be a rough passage at this particular time of the year. As soon as the last sling came aboard the hatches were covered, tarpaulins spread and wedged and the locking bars put into place. Derricks were flattened out and runners made taut. I had not known these sailors for long but they were a very good team, really hard working, and the Liverpool Bosun was popular with everyone. He could also speak the language fluently and claimed no one could beat him at the game of draughts. I believed him for he was able to wipe anyone off the board in about four moves.

As soon as we were ready for sea the sailors let go fore and aft and we went to an anchorage. The Master had received his sailing orders - which was to be 16.00 hours on 18th January.

While swinging round the anchor, the Gunlayer organised us into getting the defences into a state of readiness, as once again we would be heading into submarine infested seas, the unseen enemy. Good watch keeping was of paramount importance.

We weighed anchor and departed Bahia at 16.00 hours on 18th January 1943, joining convoy B.T.1. Total ships in convoy 28, 9 of which were bound for the U.K. The remaining 19 were for ports various. The speed of the convoy was to be 8.5 knots to Recife Brazil. Position 8 degrees

00'S.13 degrees 00 W. Thence reduce to 8 knots.

Escorts were Bahia (S.R.), Cama Quam, Cabedelo and Caravelas to Recife. Then U.S.S. Tenacity and U.S.S. Jouett.

From Recife to be relieved by Osmond Ingram

Patrol craft   P.C. - 160

" "   P.C. – 495

" "   P.C. – 575

The escort Commander was Commander Jenson U.S.S. Ericsson and U.S.S. Tenacity.

The Commodore was Lt. Commander J.E. Roberts in the Gaelic-Star.

The Vice Commodore was the Master of the S.S. Lillian Luckenbach.

We quickly discovered that one of our sister ships was in the convoy and was also bound for the U.K. so during daylight hours there was an exchange of Morse between "Gascony" and "Lombardy", not only from the Mates but also from both Masters.

Our E.T.A. for Trinidad was supposed to be 21.00 hours on January 30th. We experienced good weather and we had an efficient group of escort ships, but we were overdue, plodding along at 8 knots. However, we all made it safely and dropped anchor at Trinidad on February 2nd at 12.00 hours.

Trinidad was extremely hot but no one seemed to worry, and when possible sunbathing on No.5 hatch was the order of the day. The 'Bumboats' quickly came alongside and once again we bartered for fresh fruit. We four D.E.M.S. Gunners did a tarpaulin muster and bought a bottle of rather cheap rum. A couple of the A/B's bought a half gallon of rum as they said it would be needed when we left New York for Liverpool – winter in the North Atlantic can be very cold and rough. Originally we were bound for Halifax, Nova Scotia, but our orders had been changed by the powers that be to proceed to New York.

Apart from doing our normal fire watch duties, everyone had the pleasure of a good rest. In the morning a launch came alongside and took the Master ashore for the sailing orders. During his absence the Second Mate came along and told the Gunlayer that we were to have two extra gunners sent aboard. They turned out to be two American sailors. They were in what is called the "American Armed Guard". Trained for the defence of their Merchant ships, the equivalent of our D.E.M.S. They came aboard at about 11.00 hours and to our surprise they both had their own machine gun. A Browning point 0.05 with a portable securing stand to the ship's rail. We only had bunks for six gunners so the only thing to do was as two of us went on watch, they would take over whichever bunk was available. There was only one of them on duty at a time so it worked out.

The new gunners were young Americans who had volunteered for armed guard duties. They were not too keen on our English food, which was understandable as there was no rationing on American ships. They did tell us that their ships were 'dry' – no beer or spirits but as much Coca Cola as they wanted.

The Master was back aboard before mid-day and the news quickly circulated that we would be weighing anchor at 13.30. hours, February 3rd 1943 Convoy T.A.G. 40 consisting of 18 ships. Speed to be 9 knots to Curacao then reduced to 8 knots. Our destination was to be Guantanamo Bay, which is part of Cuba. Position 20 degrees 10' North. 75 degrees 14' West.

Our escorts were U.S.S. Biddle

P.C. (Patrol craft) P.C. 566

P.C. 567

We also had two Navy Blimps circling the convoy, as when the sea is calm and the weather clear they have the ability to see the silhouette of any submarine that may be lurking below the surface.

Commodore Ship: S.S. **Kingswood**, Captain A.W. Atkins (U.S.N. Retired)

Vice Commodore Ship: M.V. **Gaelic Star**, Lt.Commander L. Lovejoy (U.S.N. Retired)

We had a very good and uneventful passage through the Caribbean sea. E.T.A. for Guantanamo Bay was 22.00 hours on February 5th, but we arrived and anchored at 18.00 hours on February 6th. Our two American gunners from the Armed Guard were due to leave us and they quickly packed their gear and Browning machine guns. One slapped me on the back and remarked "George, you have been a good 'buddy'". He gave me five of his precious cigars to last me the rest of the trip. We helped them get their gear into the launch, gave them a wave and they were gone. I hope they survived the war.

Once again we could get a safe night's sleep. While we were at anchor it was decided that we give the 4" B.L. and 12 pounder a coat of paint. The Lamptrimmer supplied us with four good-sized paint kettles of grey paint and an assortment of brushes. Taking advantage of the hot weather, seven of us (Jock the Gunlayer, four seaman gunners and two army gunners) set to and after a full day's hard work everything was cleaned and painted, including the gun-deck, shell racks, etc. Wonder of wonders, Jock went along to the Chief Steward and bought everyone a bottle of beer!

On the morning of February 7th, an American Naval launch came alongside to collect the Master to go and receive his sailing instructions. When he returned the Second Mate told Jock that we were to be part of Convoy G.N. 40 and our estimated time of departure was to be 11.00 hours February 8th, destination New York. Our E.T.A. was 18.00 hours February 15th. We had one more night of uninterrupted sleep, which was to be our last until we made New York.

We weighed anchor at 11.00 hours on February 8th and joined up with Convoy G.N. 40. Our escorts were the U.S.S. Nourmahal, U.S.S. Impulse. P.C. 560, and P.C. 621. Commondore ship M.V. Kingswood. Total ships in convoy 33. Total speed 8 knots. Seven days steady plodding. Watches were set four on and eight off. One gunner on the gun-deck and one up in the 12 pounder pit. The weather remained good right up to the time we were abreast of Jacksonville. The barometer took a very decisive plunge and it was a quick change into cold weather gear, including duffle coats. The mood of the sea took on a sudden change. Huge waves started battering us and the wind became gale force, seeking any opening in our oilskins or duffle coats and filling them with sleet. The heavy sky came right down to the tops of the masts. For days there was not even a blink of the sun or moon or stars. The convoy plodded on. What we had encountered was a North-West gale. Visibility had fallen to zero. The Patrol Crafts were ordered to proceed at their own discretion due to severe icing conditions. U.S.S. Nourmahal reported having a cracked crankshaft in two cylinder sulzer two cycled diesel engine type R.K.H.20, for 32 kilowatt auxiliary generator. About this time, Nourmahal was ordered to withdraw on account of the gale and engine problems.

The convoy had now become dispersed and there were a lot of stragglers. By this time, Gascony was looking very pathetic from the Bridge. The North-West gale, which also brought sleet and snow, had frozen all over the for'ward derricks and the spray was freezing as it was blown over us. The Forecastle Head was one block of ice. Rails, deck and the windlass were the same. We had a list to starboard and were also down by the head. I had a bird's eye view of this as I was look-out on the starboard wing of the Bridge and all the time getting frozen into my duffle coat. Poor old Gascony had gone very sluggish – her bows were no longer lifting as they should have done. She did not appear to roll as she had been doing before this gale tore into us. I overheard the Master remark to the Second Mate that "She's performing like a lead balloon". (So I got to figuring just how does a lead balloon perform?!) I was swinging my arms together and stamping my feet to try and keep the circulation going. It was, to put it mildly, bloody cold. The Master was a man of few words, a Liverpudlian who had the respect of everyone, Officers, crew and gunners. He came over to me and said "What do you make of this lot, gunner". I could only say "My first experience, sir, of these conditions". He smiled and said "There's always a first time but more to come before we make Liverpool". He then sent his Steward round with a jug of coffee laced with rum. This was a kind gesture and put a bit of warmth into me. On February 14th the Commodore ship "M.V. Kingswood" was advised 'Delay your arrival at Ambrose until 8 hours after the E.T.A. Convoy G.N. 40 eventually arrived at Ambrose on February 16th. 27 ships in all. The 28th ship that had lost contact after the order to scatter was the "Kentuckian" which also arrived safe and sound on February 16th at Cape Henry. After passing Ambrose, we made our way into the Hudson River and anchored at 14.30 hours February 16th. The first thing the Master ordered was all hands to arm themselves with a hammer to remove the ice as quickly as possible, even chipping hammers were used and axes were borrowed from the ship's lifeboats. As it grew darker the Bosun and Lamptrimmer rigged cargo clusters from the Wheel House windows to enable us to carry on. Finally, Chippy managed to get steam through to all the winches for'ward of the Bridge and to his windlass. We also managed to warm our hands and feet on the casings.

By about 18.00 hours we had taken the list out of her and the hawse pipe was clear of the water. When we arrived we were way down by the head, the sea was just level with the bottom of the anchor on the starboard side. The Chief Mate had been working with us and he finally said "That's it lads – she will be thawed out by tomorrow morning". The Chief Steward had been ordered to give all hands a tot of rum. This quickly warmed us and gave us an appetite for our evening meal.

The main topic of conversation was whether there was going to be any shore leave. This was soon settled when the Gunlayer came down below and said he had been informed that the Master was waiting for his sailing orders so there would be no shore leave. We gazed at the Manhattan skyline in disappointment. Like the rest of my mates, I had heard so many stories about New York and longed to go and find the Stage Door Canteen, see Times Square and try American goodies.

It was still bitterly cold. We had one steam radiator in our accommodation which was about 4' long. This was in constant use to dry our socks and underclothes. It was so cold we had to keep our thick sea boots and stockings and duffle coats on at all times. We Naval gunners were very grateful for our Naval issue of John L's (hand knitted oiled wool long underpants). The ladies in the Shetland and Orkney Islands must have been kept very busy knitting for the Royal Navy. The warmest place was in our bunks. Because of the extreme cold we had been issued with an extra blanket. We also got extra rations of tea, sugar, condensed milk and cocoa.

We were swinging round the anchor until February 23rd when the Master received his sailing orders for Liverpool. We sailed at 08.00 hours that morning of Tuesday,

February 23rd. Everyone was delighted. She was a Liverpool ship and most of the Officers and crew were Liverpudlians. As soon as we headed out into the North Atlantic the North Westerly gale started clawing at us again and it was damned cold. But we were homeward bound and I had been counting the days in my diary which indicated I had been away from home for 15 months. My attitude was, to hell with the weather, please Gascony keep going and get us back to the U.K.

Other ships left the safety of the Hudson River at the same time as we did. We were all heading for W.O.M.P.'s (Western Ocean Meeting Point), position 48 degrees 28'N. 48 degrees 28 W. The convoy would be Convoy S.C. 121. The total number of ships being 64. U-Boat activity was at its worst and the Master told the Gunlayer that he wanted three look-outs on at all times – one on the 4" gun deck, one up in the 12 pounder gun-pit, and one in one of the gun-pits on the boat deck port side. The gun-pit on the starboard side was to be manned by the cadets. This meant watch and watch, 4 hours on and 4 hours off. During the hours of darkness Jock, the Gunlayer, would relieve us so that we could have a quick smoke. He would always say "Away ye go, a quick spit and a draw and a wee jam and piece"!

The Convoy of 64 ships was divided into 14 columns. When we finally got ourselves sorted out we were the leading ship of the 12th column.

Commodore ship was S.S. Bonneville (Norwegian). Commodore H.C. Birnie, R.N.R. Vice Commodore ship M.V. Empire Keats. Vice Commodore Arthur Cocks, R.N.R. Rear Commodore ship M.V. Guido.

Convoy S.C. 121 was to be escorted by the American Group A.3. Captain Heineman of the United States Coastguard Cutter Spencer. U.S.S. Destroyer Greer. Canadian Corvettes, Rosthern, Trillium, Mallow, Campion, Bibb, Babbit and H.M.S. Dianthus. H.M.S. Dauphin. Average speed to be 7.5 knots.

The weather was now West South West, gale 8 – 9 and a high sea. Snow storms and bad weather generally deteriorating.

After departing W.O.M.P.'s the assembly point, there was no let up in the weather conditions. The North Atlantic was really living up to its reputation. The cargo we were carrying – manganese ore in every hold - made conditions aboard much worse. We were rolling heavily and taking heavy spray aboard. The bows started to plunge deep into the sea, taking water up the hawse pipe and spraying it over the forecastle, then disappearing over the Forecastle Head in a mass of froth into the rising sea. The sky had taken on that ominous grey pallor with touches of yellow and black streaks that only an Atlantic gale foreshadows. The wind gradually increasing in crescendo with its passage though the masts, stays and funnel guys. We were plunging and rolling heavily. As the waves crashed against the stem the spray had turned into a mass of green sea; roaring over the Forecastle Head and down onto No. 1 hatch covers, the foaming torrents sweeping over the locking bars, down over the coamings, and then crashing onto the fore deck and out the lea scuppers, only to be sucked up by the wind and blown like mares tails into the sea below. The constant flurries of snow and spray had made visibility very poor.

My lookout post was in the gun-pit on the port side of the boat deck. I became a snowman, one human block of frozen sleet then snow. The tiny scupper at the bottom of the gun-pit was either too small, not designed for these conditions, or some idiot had left a lump of cotton waste in the pit when cleaning the machine gun. The result was I was sloshing about in sea water which further added to my problems. When one of the Stewards came round with a mug of coffee, I said "Go and tell the Gunlayer to bring a piece of wire along and clean this .... scupper out before I drown in this ... waterlogged pit". He got the message and it turned out that a lump of greasy cotton waste had lodged there.

As the ship rises on the crest of a wave, then plunges downwards into the gigantic trough of the sea, the single screw thrashes widely at where the sea is supposed to be, just momentarily, but long enough to send out its signal of distress. She starts to rise again and the seas come crashing aboard the weather-side and goes crashing down the working alleyways as she continues to roll and plunge as the wind increases and makes the sounds like a hundred banshees screaming through the stays and guys. Even the aerial has taken on a scream where it passes the insulation into the radio shack from the mast above. Down in the galley, the clatter of pots and pans various creates a din all of their own, accompanied by the yells of the galley staff trying desperately to secure them. As we continue this cork-screw motion through the sea, accompanied by the never ending thrashing of the screw, the steel box-beams that run fore and aft throughout the vessel creak and groan like a demon in distress, as each one gives its allotted stretch to enable the vessel's stress to cope with the tons of pressure that is straining the hull to its extremity. You stop to wonder, "Did the draughts-men and rivetters do their job?", knowing, of course, the 'Yard' she was built in and their past record.

The boats in their davits groan up against their puddings and the relieving tackle made fast, but ready to be launched by giving the senhouse slip a hefty clout with the hammer made fast alongside it, should the need arise. The gunner and cadet keeping a lookout in our circular gun-pits on the after end of the boat deck were being subjected to the continual lashing of spray and blinding snow. The fiddley skylights were clamped tight down to prevent any spray or sea finding its way down into the Engine Room. The lookouts on the 4" gun deck and 12 pounder pit had to brace them-selves secure by bracing themselves onto any form of solid support, like-wise the lookouts on the wings of the Bridge. The Helmsman had to jam or brace himself between the binnacle and the telemotor.

On occasions like this the wheel had to be gripped until one's knuckles became white. The zig-zag clock gives out its roar, meaning a change of course should the Master agree. But encountering a sea such as this, zig-zagging was out of the question. The vessel's head was now with sea roughly three points on the bow. The wind still howls, but a wee bit more comfort now as speed has been reduced. We still plunge and cannot rid ourselves of the corkscrew motion with wind and spray, water disappearing from the decks in sheets of green as she rises again.

The Master has somehow jammed himself in front of the Kent clearview screen and surveys the decks again. What, if any, damage did that last wave do to my ship? What course can I safely alter to, to ease the strain on her? But three points on the bow have it and we try to keep it there. The wind still howls and the creeks continue. Days of these conditions tire everyone aboard with sleepless nights. We have to wedge ourselves into our bunks to prevent being cast out onto the deck. When we gunners go below decks after our four hours in the gun pit, all we remove is our Mae West and iced up duffle coat. We have whatever food is available and crash down on top of our bunks with our sea boots on. We all sensed that we were in for a rough passage, including U-Boats, but thank goodness I had, by now, overcome my seasickness and could even enjoy a cigarette again.

The Atlantic gale continues on, coming down on us from the "Bismark-Straits" between Greenland and Iceland, with a bit of wind from Labrador. With an icy touch this continued for days with submarines ahead of the convoy preparing for their onslaught.

The wave patterns in the Atlantic are with swell approximately 2 medium, thence the third one is usually of much greater height and furore.

The Pacific Ocean is normally 4 medium and the fifth being much larger, but one cannot wait to judge these sequences to get a lifeboat away in war conditions or any emergency. Time is vital to save lives.

The type of zig-zag can be varied to confuse the enemy. The Convoy Commodore or Senior Escort will decide and advise all ships in his convoy of its number by Morse lamp. All ships would then follow this pattern. The object is twofold. Firstly, to make it difficult for the U-boats to get into a firing position, and secondly to confuse their aiming and anticipated track and arrival of their torpedoes.

The zig-zag clocks were very similar to the Chartroom round brass clocks, except that they had an ear-piercing ring which could be quite startling if one was not fully prepared for it. It was usually placed in the bulkhead behind the Helmsman. This ear-piercing zig-zag clock was a standing joke amongst both Officers and seamen. It was said that it would give away our position and the U-boats would hear it.

"What we are about to face"

The allied U-boat situation maps from March 1st to 6th, based on Special Intelligence and D/F locations, showed a massing of U-boat groups on the Northern convoy route, their numbers climbing from 31 to 49. Between Newfoundland and Greenland there lay in wait for S.C. 121 the two groups "Burggraf and Wildfang" with a total of 24 U-boats in dog-leg patrol line. Behind the patrol line, 7 more U-Boats were lying in wait, but in the prevailing heavy storms not all the boats were apparently in their intended positions; with the result that the Convoy, which was to some extent widely scattered and behind which many stragglers were following, passed the patrol line unobserved on March 5th.

Only at 09.56 hours on the next day did one of the U-boats waiting behind the patrol line, the U.405 (Kpt. Hopmann) find the S.C. 121 which consisted originally of 64 ships divided into 14 columns, escorted by Captain Heinman, United States Coastguard Cutter "Spencer".

The U-boat Commander deployed against this convoy 'The Westmark Group' consisting of the following U-boats: U.405, U.409, U.591, U.230, U.228, U.566, U.616, U.448, U.526, U.634, U.527, U.659, U.523, U.709, U.359, U.332, U.432.

At the same time, he ordered U.229, U.665, U.447, U.190, U.439, U.530, U.618 and U.642, which were within range and were proceeding to their new patrol line, 'Neuland' envisaged for March 8[th,] to form another patrol line 'Ostmark' on the suspected convoy route.

The contact signals from U.405 were located by H.F./D.F. equipment on "Spencer" with the result that U.405 was driven off.

We continued on our various courses but by this time there were a lot of stragglers, or rompers as the U-Boat captain named them.

On Saturday, March 6th, submarines reported in the vicinity at noon: noon position 55 degrees 35' N. 39 degrees 20' West. Bad stragglers due to snowstorms and bad weather.

Saturday, March 6th at 20.40 hours a ship on the port wing column fired two white rockets and reported by W/T that a submarine was passing ahead on the outside of the column. The visibility was two miles.

Saturday, March 6th, 23.49 hours. The Egyptian, No. 61, second ship in the sixth column, was struck by a torpedo on the starboard side by the U.230, the Commander was Seigmann. She was 2,868 tons and sank in latitude 56 degrees 25' N. 37 degrees 38 W. She was attacked and sank in the darkness of the night. In the morning the U.230 attacked another ship in the Egyptian's former position. It is possible that both targets were the same ship. The escort and most ships were unaware that she had gone down. No further activity or enemy reports this night.

Sunday, March 7th, at 09.06 hours. The Empire Impala, No. 25, fifth ship in the second column, was torpedoed by the U.591. Commander was Zetsche. She was 6,116 tons and sank in Latitude 58 degrees N, 15 degrees W. Note: The Empire Impala had hove to in order to pick up survivors from the Egyptian, and the U.591 attacked and sank her. Sadly, there were only three survivors.

Sunday, March 7th, at 15.43 hours. No. 115, Clune Park, the fifth ship in the eleventh column, reported a submarine on the port beam of convoy at 15.58. The submarine submerged and at 16.09 hours Clune Park reported submarine attacking. Weather, westerly gales, high seas with snow and squals.

During the first night attack on the convoy, and also during subsequent night attacks, the order to fire was what we called Snowflakes. The shells were fired from the escort ship. I cannot say at what height they detonated but when they burst it created a huge cascade of white light, just like a giant firework. The result was startling when seen for the first time. It was like a giant searchlight descending upon us, lighting up the whole convoy. But the main object was to spot any submarine that had the nerve to surface – and they did.

March 7th at 15.30 hours. The Fort Lamy, No.34 the fourth ship in the third column, was torpedoed by the U.527. Commander was Uhlig. She was 5,242 tons and carrying TNT in the forward hold. She sank in latitude 58 degrees 30' N, 31 degrees 00 W. The Fort Lamy was also carrying on deck one very large L.C.T. (Landing Craft Tank) L.C.T.-2480 preparing for the invasion. There was also a second one on the Commodore ship. They weighed 143 tons. Three survivors were picked up.

Monday, March 8th. Noon position 58 degrees 14' N. 30 degrees 05' W. At 01.30 hours two detonations heard astern of convoy. At 13.10 hours W/T message intercepted from No. 22 Vojvoda Putnik (Yugoslavian) that she was sinking. No information why. This message was made with variations several times. At 14.02 hours aircraft made by R/T "am attacking submarine 247 degrees 11 miles from convoy".

Monday, March 8th at 16.21 hours. The Vojvoda Putnik, the second ship in the second column No. 22, was torpedoed by the U.591. Commander was Zetzsche. She was 5,879 tons and was sunk in latitude 58 degrees 42' N. 31 degrees 25' W. She carried a full load of wheat.

Note: The Vojvoda Putnik had been straggling with steering difficulties since morning. No record of casualties.

We had No 120 squadron R.A.F. and U.S.N. squadron 84 operating from Iceland, giving us protective sweeps for both convoy O.N. 170 and convoy S.C. 121. Aircraft used were Flying Fortresses, Liberators and Sunderlands. They used depth charges.

The weather now was gale force 10 with many snow and hail showers and there were some recording of winds up to 132 m.p.h.

Monday, March 8th. Noon position 58 degrees 14' N. 30 degrees 5' West. Weather W.S.W. Rough sea. At 19.00 hours heavy depth charge detonations heard on starboard bow of convoy. At 19.20 hours "Kingswood" No.31, the first ship in column 6, reported by W/T a torpedo passing her port bow. At 19.22 hours the same ship reported submarine passed ahead to port. Believed to have rammed her. Oerlikon tracer observed falling close to port bow of No.51 from a quarterly direction. No.51 was the lead ship in column No.5, the "Empire Keats" Vice Commodore ship.

March 8th at 08.55 hours. The Guido had wandered away from the convoy and was 10 nautical miles off the starboard bow of the convoy. The German U-boat Commander referred to her as "a romper". She was torpedoed by the U.526. Commander was Moglich. She was 3,921 tons and was sunk in latitude 58 degrees 08 N. 32 degrees 20' West. The United States coastguard cutter Spencer made Asdic contact and attacked with depth charges. Result unknown. Guido had started out as Rear Commodore and was the lead ship in the 11th column No. 111 until she wandered away to starboard of the convoy. Spencer picked up 31 survivors, including the Master, but there were 14 unaccounted for.

March 8th at 21.55 hours. The Empire Lakeland No. 141, the lead ship in the 14th column, was torpedoed by the U.190. Commander was Wintermeyer. She was 7,015 tons and was sunk in latitude 58 degrees N. 15 degrees W. The U.190 sank a lone vessel with two torpedoes, a straggler they assumed was the Empire Lakeland. I was on watch when she was torpedoed. Ahead of us on the starboard bow I reported three red Mae West lights floating down our starboard side. The look-out on the starboard wing of the Bridge and the cadet in the starboard gun-pit also saw them. It was assumed that the Empire Lakeland had somehow got out of position and been struck by the torpedo intended for the Gascony.

March 8th at 23.03 hours. The Leadgate (no column number given), was torpedoed by the U.642. Commander was Brunning. She was 2,125 tons and sank in latitude 58 degrees N. 15 degrees W. There were no survivors. The Leadgate was a straggler and should have sailed with convoy H.S.C. 121.

March 9th at 21.36 hours. The Milos, No.64, was the fourth ship in the sixth column. She was torpedoed by the U.530. The Commander was Lange. She was 3,058 tons and was torpedoed in latitude 58 degrees N. 15 degrees W. Records say the U.530 sank a lone vessel and Milos was a straggler. She was a Swedish ship.

The gale force winds, accompanied by hail and snow showers, still persisted. The Gunlayer had been on the Bridge after the sighting of the red Mae West lights floating past us on the starboard side. No one heard cries for help so it was assumed they had all died in the icy cold seas. The Master said they would have been lucky to survive half an hour in these conditions. Being continually exposed to snow and hail and sloshing about in the gun-pit the cold had started to affect my legs and knees. At that time no sailor ever carried any form of painkillers. I saw the Second Mate who from the ship's medical chest gave me sufficient tablets to last three days. I do not know what they were but they did help to alleviate most of the pain. The pain persisted and after three days I was back for more.

March 9th at 21.28 hours. The Malantic, an American ship, No. 102 and the second ship in the tenth column, was torpedoed by the U.409. Commander was Massman. She was 3,837 tons and was torpedoed in latitude 58 degrees 37' N. 22 degrees 32' W. The U.409 says the ship sunk after one hit. The Malantic sank in 15 minutes. Radar and Asdic very ineffective due to sea conditions. There were only 21 survivors, 25 unaccounted for.

March 9th. 09.30 hours to 10.30 hours. Heavy depth charge and detonations heard astern. Weather W.S.W. gale 8 to 9 and high seas.

At 19.20 hours the Rarranga, No.113 and the third ship in the 11th column, reports by R/T suspicious object on starboard side between the columns, possibly a submarine. No firing heard.

19.46 hours. Forward screen of escorts. Fires star shell.

19.53 hours. Loud detonations.

22.10 hours. Two white rockets from the starboard column leading ship. This was later presumed to be "Bonneville" the Commodore ship.

22.20 hours. No. 51, Vice Commodore ship Empire Keats passed close to sinking ships, Nos. 23 and 24. Reported they had been very much ahead of their stations.

22.27 hours. No. 51, Empire Keats, fired one 4" round. Red 50 degrees range 500 yards, at an object low in the water.

March 9th. 21.45 hours. The Rosewood, No. 74 and the 4th ship in the 7th column. She was torpedoed by the U.409. Commander Massman. She was 5,989 tons and was torpedoed in Lat. 58 degrees 37 N. 22 degrees 32 W.

Note: The U.409 torpedoed the Rosewood which broke in two and was finally sunk by the Coastguard Cutter Bibb. One other detonation was also heard. The Rosewood was a tanker loaded with A.D. fuel for the Clyde. I was on watch when she went up. She was way over on our port quarter. Her bow and stern remained afloat but was later sank by gunfire. Position 58 degrees 36'N. 20 degrees 12 W. There were no survivors.

March 10th. 00.07 hours. The Bonneville, a Norwegian ship, was No. 81 and the leading ship in the eighth column. She was torpedoed by U.405. Commander was Hopmann. She was 4,665 tons and was torpedoed in latitude 58 degrees 45 N. 21 degrees 57' W. She was carrying on deck an L.C.T. – 2341 landing craft tank weighing 143 tons. (Note: The U.405

observed two hits from starboard on one ship which sank. From Allied sources, it is learned that the Bonneville was sunk at the time of U.229's attack, but this boat attacked from the port side and Bonneville was hit on the starboard side.)

Confidential papers were thrown overboard in a weighted box. She sank very quickly in 15 minutes with all hands abandoning. One report states 38 missing and 13 known dead. Two survivors were rescued by the Cutter Bibb from the foremost raft which drifted from the vessel. The Commodore and the Ship's Master were unable to reach the raft after jumping into the water. She had a crew of 40 and 8 in the Commodore's staff.

NOTE After the tragic loss of Commodore Birnie and his ship, the Vice Commodore, Arthur Cocks, R.N.R., took over on his ship "The Empire Keats". The Rear Commodore's ship, M.V. Guido, had already been sunk. At this stage I cannot say who and which ship became Vice Commodore. We all got to know that we had lost the Commodore ship because we knew her position. I was very sad because I had sailed with Commodore Birnie on a previous North Atlantic crossing. (Convoy H.X. 142, August 1st 1941 Halifax to Liverpool. He was then the Vice Commodore in the "Lock Ewe".)

It was during this horrendous weather that we were very nearly capsized by a giant wave. Freak or not I shall never know, but I had been relieved off the 4 – 8 a.m. watch. Had my breakfast and we were really performing. I decided to have a break when there was a deafening thud that shook the whole ship from stem to stern. We all thought we had been struck by a torpedo. We had been struck on the starboard side by what must have been a gigantic wave and we were literally lying on our port side just shuddering as the screw was thrashing around slicing the air. Our first and foremost thought was self-preservation. Get up and on to the deck. I never took my sea boots off whether on or off watch but I had removed my Mae West and wet duffle coat. I put them back on in a flash and like the rest made a dash for the stairway. We were met with a torrent of ugly green frothy sea which just simply poured down into our accommodation. The same sea had smashed its way through a thick 2" wooden alleyway door leading to the Engineer Officers accommodation. It just smashed like plywood. The sailors were all out and the Bosun said "the bloody cargo has shifted". I did not know at that time but when they load manganese ore it is loaded in the form of a pyramid. The severe weather and the huge wave had moved it and piled it all on the port side, giving us this terrible list. The two gunners in the boat deck gun-pits were literally clinging on for their lives. I was to understand this after the war when I was studying for my tickets that we had very nearly lost our stability "metacentric height". Another shift of cargo and we would have been over and down into the "Bosun's Locker". However, a miracle happened and it did not take very long. Somehow another sea bore down on us and this time it struck the port side, moved the cargo again and we became upright and back on an even keel. It was a really terrifying time for everyone. All we had to do was to get down below and bail all the seawater out of the accommodation and dump it into the loo. Only one dry gunner and that was Jock Andrews, the gunlayer who had a cabin way up on the poop. When he went on to the Bridge to report what had happened, the Master said "We shall remember this one". The worst weather in the North Atlantic on record for 60 years.

March 10th. 00.05 hours. The Nailsea Court. She was No. 3. The 3rd ship in the 2nd column. She was torpedoed by the U. 229. Commander Schetelig. She was 4,964 tons and was torpedoed in Lat. 58 degrees 45'N. 21 degrees 57' West. Judging from the running times of the torpedoes, the hits from the U.229 must all have been in the first and second columns. But the Commodore Ship Bonneville was in position No. 81, lead ship column 8., so she must have been struck by U.405. She was abandoned and sank quickly. There were only three survivors and 45 unaccounted for.

After the fifth attack, a large oil slick was seen on the surface and a piece of wood in the middle of it.

March 10th. 00.07 hours. The Coulmore. She was No. 24, the 4th ship in the 2nd column. She was torpedoed by the U.229. Commander Schetelig. She was 3,670 tons and was torpedoed in Latitude 58 degrees 48'N. 22 degrees 00' W.

Note: The Coulmore was abandoned too quickly and was still afloat at 16.37 hours on Thursday, 11th March. A tug was dispatched to salvage her. There were seven survivors and 36 unaccounted for. A great pity that the order to abandon ship was given resulting in such a great loss of sailors. However, decisions had to be made as soon as the torpedo struck, just a matter of minutes and no trace was very often the case. The good news was that an Admiralty Report released on 22nd March stated Coulmore torpedoed. Arrived in tow. Damaged off Oversay. The U. 229, Commander Schetelig, surfaced between the columns he torpedoed. The Nailsea Court at 00.05 hours March 10th, third ship, 2nd column. Lat 58 degrees 45'N. 21 degrees 57 West, then at 00.07 hours March 10th he torpedoed The Coulmore, fourth ship, 2nd column. Lat. 58 degrees 48'N. 22 degrees 00' West. Both ships in same column and only 3 minutes difference in latitude and 3 minutes in longitude. The Coulmore was taken in tow on the 11th March and they made it back to U.K.

March 10th. 11.15 hours. The Scorton. She was No. 52, the second ship in the 5th column. She was in the position to ram a submarine at 08.30 hours. Then she was attacked by the U.229. Grid reference A.L. 2622. The U.229 heard detonations after 2 minutes 45 seconds and 4 minutes 15 seconds. The Freighter Scorton in position No. 52 saw a torpedo that had missed her. The U.616, Commander Koitschna, heard a detonation after 6 minutes 40 seconds but this was a depth charge dropped by H.M.C.S. Dianthus. (Her Majesty's Canadian Ship).

March 10th. Noon positions of the convoy but not stragglers and rompers, was 50 degrees 49'N. 19 degrees 00 West. At 03.36 hours an R/T to "Empire Keats" from the Senior Escort reads "Commodore" has been lost. You are to take over. "Empire Keats" was No. 51, lead ship Column 5. Vice Commodore Arthur Cocks, R.N.R. At daylight, 35 Merchant ships in company. Reformed into seven columns at the request of the Ocean Escorts, Captain Heineman of the United States Coast Guard Cutter "Spencer". When we assembled and began our Eastward passage from W.O.M.P.S. there had been a total of 64 ships. Some had returned to various ports with engine trouble. There had been numerous stragglers and rompers. Up to and including the 10th March, we had lost a total of 12 ships. The Coulmore, which had been abandoned had been taken in tow by a tug. Reported arrived at Oversay.

14.30 Starboard bow escort Black Pennant

14.35 Starboard bow escort depth charging

14.37 Emergency turn to port

14.58 Resumed course

Senior escort signalled "Dianthus" made good attack and has now lost contact.

18.47 Heavy detonations presumed depth charges

18.50 "   "   "   "   "

19.19 "   "   "   "   "   "

19.48 "   "   "   "   "   "

20.24 Rear ship of 3rd column from port wing made two series of six blasts. No W/T. This was reported to S.O. escort by R/T but no answer was received.

Evasive steering was carried out during the nights of 6th – 10th March, courses being altered away from the mean line of advance just previous to darkness and back to line of advance before dawn.

After the last attack, by orders from Captain Heineman, United States Coastguard Cutter "Spencer", the convoy is reformed into 35 ships and eleven columns. The storm once again increased to force 10 with the result that attacks attempted by the U.229 (Schetelig), the U.616 (Kojtschka), U.523 (Pietsch), U.642 (Brunning) and U. 634 (Dahlaus), all failed and the stragglers they encountered could not be attacked because of the weather. The last contact keeper, the U. 634, was finally driven off in the afternoon.

In these operations the escorts were impeded because the weather made it impossible to use the radio and radar equipment and because of storm damage.

Analysis During February and March 1943, convoys S.C. 121, H.X. 228, S.C. 122 and H.X. 229. These four consecutive eastbound transatlantic convoys were all heavily attacked. It was estimated that possibly as many as 70 U boats operated against them. The total escort provided to cover them consisted of 23 ships with a further 15 ships who were present for only part of the time. On average, the escorts were outnumbered by U-boats about two to one. A total of 30 ships were torpedoed in the convoy.

There were quite a lot of stragglers, one of which left the convoy deliberately. 155 ships arrived safely. S.C. 121 already had three stragglers when the Ocean escort took over, but with continuous south-westerly and westerly gales that persisted from the 4th to 12th March, the number had been increased to sixteen. The remaining ships that remained in the convoy also became scattered and due to the rough weather the Senior officer was unable to have the number of columns reduced from fourteen to eleven as he wished until after the main attacks on the convoy took place.

Note from Admin. This horrendous weather that we all had to encounter undoubtedly reduced the efficiency of the escorts detecting devices. This handicap was also increased by breakdowns. To quote the Senior Officer stating "At one time two or three H/F, D/F sets were inoperative, similarly four of the eight escorts had their radars out of commission, while the Asdic sets of three of the eight ships present were defective. R/T communication also appears to have been unreliable. During daylight hours on 9th March, a number of H/F transmissions were D/F'd, but for various reasons full value in appreciating the U-boats dispositions was not obtained. Chief among these were the endeavours being made at this time. To home in on Trillium, one of the escorts who had lost touch and also four escorts joining us from Iceland. Coastguard Cutter "Spencer" also experienced difficulty in obtaining the sense of her bearings and it is stated that the performance of Greer's H/F, D/F (High frequency direction finder) was erratic. During this period, H.M.C.S. "Rostern" (Corvette) who was on the starboard beam expended forty-four depth charges in a series of seven promising attacks. A large oil slick was seen with a piece of wood floating in the middle of it. The U-boats made a number of successful attacks. Apart from these, a number of attempted attacks were frustrated by offensive action on the part of the escort.

I stayed on at sea after the war until 1969, and as I travelled around the world I encountered some very angry seas, but I never experienced anything to match the gales of 1943.

Of the five attacks, the heaviest appeared to be on the nights of the 8th, 9th and 10 March, roughly thirty-six hours after the convoy had first been escorted – though weakly – by aircraft. I say this with the greatest of respect for the aircrews. They had a very difficult and dangerous job to carry out owing to the widely scattered state of the convoy. 64 ships in 14 columns covered a huge area of ocean.

Analysis of air cover from Iceland   Classified

March 7th 08.28 hours.   Flying Fortress No. 8/220 "sighted" U-boat 30 degrees to starboard of convoy.   Attacked with 7 depth charges.

March 8th 15.53 hours.   Liberator No. R/120 "sighted" U-boat 11 degrees starboard quarter.   Attacked with 4 depth charges.

March 8th Same Liberator "sighted" U-boat 25 degrees astern.   Attacked with 2 depth charges.

March 10th 12.40 hours.   Short Sunderland No. 2302 "sighted" U-boat 70 degrees starboard beam.   U-boat dived too quickly to be depth charged.

March 7th. 07.56 hours.   The "Miguell-da-Larrinaga" – a straggler - 72 miles astern of convoy reported a torpedo passing her starboard bow.

March 7th. 17.30 hours.   The "Clune Park" – a straggler – 24 miles astern of convoy in position 57 degrees 34' N. 35 degrees 22' W, reported 'have engaged the enemy during a South West gale and high seas who submerged, then no further contact."

A.D.M. report to S.C. 121   The "Miguell-da-Larrinaga" and "Clune Park" reported stragglers

March 8th. 15.00 hours.   A.D.M. to S.C. 121.   Position course and speed. Position 58 degrees 36'N. 30 degrees 05' W.   Course 90 degrees, speed 7.25 knots.

At 21.25 hours on March 8th – course 63 degrees.

At 05.15 hours on March 9th – course 90 degrees

All 44 scattered.   5 escorts.

March 8th.   S.C. 121 to A.D.M.   Two U-boats sighted 19.40 hours and 20.40 hours mean position abeam.   Aircraft and Spencer attacking with depth charges.

March 8th. 08.10 hours.   No. 111 Guido – straggler – 10 miles on starboard bow.   Torpedoed and sunk.   Spencer made Asdic contact and attacked with depth charges. Result unknown. 31 survivors, including Master, aboard Spencer. 14 unaccounted for.

March 5<u>th.</u> S.C. 121 51 degrees 28' N. 45 degrees 45' West. Convoy scattered on account of bad weather.

March 6<u>th.</u> To escort convoy S.C. 121, U-boat position by D.F. at 12.15 hours on the 6<u>th</u>. Within 150 miles of 55 degrees 30' N. 38 degrees West. 13768 KCS B.T. type.

March 6<u>th.</u> To escort convoy S.C. 121, urgent U-boat warning. U-boat estimated in your vicinity by D.F. at 10.14 hours. Has made a sighting report of a convoy or important unit. X. 7770 KCS. B.E.P. within 150 miles of 53 degrees 30' N. 38 degrees 30' West.

March 7<u>th</u>. Submarine sighted and attacked by Spencer at 11.20 hours on 7<u>th</u>. Convoy S.C. 121 position 57 degrees 05' N. 36 degrees 40' West at 058 degrees. Speed 7.5 knots.

March 8<u>th</u>. Submarine sighted at 17.30 hours in position 37 degrees 34' N. 35 degrees 22' West.

March 8<u>th</u>. U-boat position by D/F at 01.15 hours within 100 miles 57 degrees N. 37 degrees West. Enigma 77 group.

March 8<u>th</u> Admin. S.C. 121 widely scattered steering due to Westerly gale. Some ships hove to. 54 ships present this cipher 19.00 hours 8/3/43 position 57 degrees 45' N. 34 degrees 14' West. Speed 7.5 knots. Estimated course 075 degrees.

March 11<u>th</u>. Report from BIBS in position 58 degrees 30' N. 21 degrees 00' West. Have located after half of unarmed tanker. Port and starboard lifeboats not launched. No sign of life aboard. Am searching to windward of course 290 degrees for possible survivors.

March 11<u>th</u> U.S.S. Babbitt and Ingram report ships escorting convoy S.C. 121 returning to Reykjavic. Convoy considered no longer threatened.

March 11<u>th</u> D.F. Bearing on 77-70 KCS at 17.11 hours indicate convoy was probably being reported by U-boats.

March 14<u>th</u> Spencer, Greer, Dianthus, Rosthem, Dauphin and Trillium arrived safe back in Reykjavic after escorting convoy S.C. 121.

March 9<u>th</u>. 20.35 hours position 58 degrees 37'N. 24 degrees 20'West.

Bibbs, Ingram, Babbit joined. 44 ships considerably scattered. 7 escorts 1 rejoining. 4 sightings. 1 attempted attack late night. 3 attempted attacks today. Majority close. Aboard convoy. Work by escorts. Superb.

H.M.S. Harvester "picked up, going by record," 50 seamen and was then diverted to go and assist another convoy which had come under attack. Convoy H.X. 228. She herself got torpedoed by the U.43 (Commander Eckhart) on March 11th. Position 51 degrees 23 N. 28 degrees 40' West, and unfortunately all 50 perished. H.M.S. Harvester was a Destroyer of 1,340 tons.

It has proved very difficult to find the exact number of seamen who lost their lives in convoy S.C. 121, but the severe mauling we suffered during the five attacks, one could, without contradiction, say we may have lost more seamen than in any of the other convoys. The gale force winds, along with sleet, hail and snow, severely hampered. Total tonnage of the twelve ships lost was 55,965. G.R.T. This includes the two L.C.T.'s being carried on deck. One on the Commodore ship "Bonneville" and one on the deck of the "Fort Lamy".

On Wednesday, March 10th, welcomed reinforcements reached us. Two Corvettes, H.M.S. "Campion" and H.M.S. "Mallow". On March 11th, because the convoy was approaching the "North Channel", the operation was broken off early by "the Commander U-boats". According to records, the German C-in-C U-boats, Kaarl-Donitz, deployed 221 U-boats in the North Atlantic during the month of February, and 231 during the month of January 1943. We were unaware at the time of the tactics that Donitz and his Commanders used to deploy his Wolf Packs against the continual and never ending number of Merchant ships that were convoyed, both westbound and east-bound across the Atlantic by the Royal Navy. Thank you all and everyone. Not forgetting our American and Canadian cousins along with the war ships from the Allied countries who joined us. So on the 11th March when the attacks were called off, the U-boats turned round and headed westwards to regroup and refuel from their ocean-going Submarine Tankers, then position themselves to attack and maul yet another convoy.

H.M.S. "Watchman" and H.M.S. "Rockingham" relieved U.S.S. Babbitt in position 62 degrees 01'N. 24 degrees 00' West at 14.15 hours, then proceeded to join convoy S.C. 121 at 16 knots. E.T.A. 08.00 hours March 9th.

Thursday, March 11th at 11.03 hours convoy S.C. 121 is no longer considered threatened. Escorts U.S.S. Babbitt and Ingham ordered to return to Reykjavic.

Friday, March 12th. H.M.S. "Trillium" reports her fuel situations getting critical and is ordered to proceed to Londonderry. Refuelling at sea was made extremely difficult, or nigh impossible, on account of the horrendous weather and sea conditions prevailing at the time.

Saturday, March 13th. At 04.27 hours convoy S.C. 121, consisting of 21 ships, was met by local escort H.M.S. "Kirkella" 55 degrees 24' N. 06 degrees 22' West, course 117 degrees, speed 7.5 knots. Ocean escort was relieved at 05.10 hours March 13th and to Londonderry. H.M.S. "Mallow" to Liverpool.

The weather began to get warmer and the sea started to get much calmer. We had the short Sunderlands out to escort us to the safety of our point of arrival Oversay. One of the Sunderlands, as if to give us all a treat, came down to nearly mast high. All hands out on deck to give them a wave and some of the ships sounded their sirens.

As soon as we got into the North Channel and left Rathlin Island astern, the Master told Jock (our Gunlayer) to stop the watch and watch which we had been on since we sailed from New York on 23rd February. So after 18 days of double watches, we all drew a breath of relief and a few hours extra sleep. At the first opportunity I went along and saw the Second Mate and got a further supply of painkillers.

Just before we were abreast of Belfast, one of ships astern of us altered her course and hauled round to starboard heading for Belfast. She had a torpedo caught up in her nets which had failed to explode. This was discovered when they raised the booms, which was lucky for them. The most important thing was that we now had plenty of water as at certain times we could only draw fresh water from a tap amidships abaft the galley. Then a padlock was clamped on it. My first and last experience of that particular kind of saving fresh water!!

The shower went back on in our cramped accommodation, off came the 'Long Johns' – beginning to get a bit smelly as they had had to stay on since we sailed from New York. The hot shower and shave worked wonders and the food tasted better. For some unknown reason there was more of it. After a real hot breakfast and a couple of painkillers, it was into my bunk for real – the first time since February 23rd. The only thing I ever removed during that time was my duffle coat as it was always wet, the Mae-West came off but quickly went back on again.

The weather had got much kinder. The sea had flattened out and the sun finally shone down upon us. When we passed the I.O.M., leaving it to port, I had recollections of passing once before when I sailed from the Clyde in convoy W.S. 15 on January 10th 1942. The first and foremost tasks that beset us now was to give all the armaments a good clean and slightly grease or oil, canvas covers on, 4" and 12 pounder shells stowed away. We were a good team and the sooner all these jobs were completed the sooner we could get our kit-bags packed.

While I was working on the machine guns on the wings of the Bridge, the Third Mate told me the sad new that the Master had received news that his son had been killed in the Fleet Air Arm. We were all very saddened to hear this as the Master had been a tower of strength to all his crew in getting us through those horrendous seas, not forgetting the U-boats, or as the Bosun remarked one day "They are like shoals of bloody herrings". I thought this was a good one and it cheered me up a wee bit. I was thankful we had some "Scousers" aboard, they always came up with some funny quotes.

After satisfying the Gunlayer that all the armaments were cleaned and securely covered, we had time to pack our kit-bags. My first job was to unroll my hammock and stow 200 duty-free Players and ½ pound of tobacco. I thought I would be entitled to some leave so to take home I had bought some tins of food. We were allowed 5 lbs of rationed goods and most sailors got whatever they could afford. I also had some rice and had saved my chocolate ration.

All I had to declare was six pairs of Nylon stockings – which were much in demand! We docked at Liverpool and made fast during the early hours of March 17th. After breakfast I bade farewell to the Master and Mates, also the Chief Engineers for keeping the engines turning over - not even one minutes problem since the day I signed on. After what we had experienced as a team during those days and nights at the mercy of Donitz's U-boat packs, I and the rest of the gunners seemed reluctant to leave Gascony. After 15 months and 22 days it was hard to realise that we were finally back in England.

The D.E.M.S. Officer was aboard just after 09.00 hours. He quickly satisfied himself that everything was OK and informed us that transport would be alongside at 10.30 hours. We piled our gear into a sling and the dockers landed it on the wharf. As I started to go down the gangway, something made me stop. I don't know what it was. I raised my hand and gave the fishplate a good hard slap and said "Thank you Gascony for getting me home". It is amazing how one gets to be part of a ship and develops a sentimental attachment to her. Gascony survived the war and continued to work for "Royal Mail Lines" until 1958 when she was sold and went to the breakers yard.

We got taken to D.E.M.S. barracks and were informed that we had to take all our gear home – 2 kit-bags, a hammock and a suitcase. Then it was transport to Lime Street Station, deposit our gear in the left luggage and down to Liver Buildings for a railway warrant and leave pay. I was awarded 28 days leave so I collected the balance of my wages and leave pay which amounted to quite a few pounds.

Before leaving I decided to see the R.N. Medical Offcer for his opinion about the state of my legs for which I was taking painkillers. His advice was to keep my feet dry and warm and that I would fare much better if I could get a ship that sailed into warmer climates. He gave me a month's supply of tablets and said I should see the M.O. before I signed on my next ship.

I quickly got a taxi back to Lime Street station and got the first available train through to Chesterfield. I arrived home during the afternoon when the children were at school and my Uncle was working in the fields. It was good to have a good long talk with my Aunt over some tea and home made cakes. It was bread-making day and there was a lovely smell of freshly baked bread - it was really great to be home again!

Names of Master, Officers, Crew and Gunners of M.V. "GASCONY"

H.G. Whittle	Master
L.J. Peterson	Chief Officer
C. Robertson	Second Officer
R. English	Third Officer
J.E. Bridges	Apprentice
W.M. Morton	Apprentice
R. Hamilton	Chief Engineer
J.L. Dingwall	Second Engineer
R.G. Blackwell	Third Engineer
R. Rae	Fourth Engineer
L.J. Moth	Junior Engineer
A. Stockton	Junior Engineer
T. Williams	Junior Engineer
E.J. Hart	Electrician
D.G. Mitchell	Captain's Clerk
G. Manson	First Radio Officer
G. Unsworth	Second Radio Officer
T.C.L. Jones	Third Radio Officer
A. Towers	Boatswain and Lamptrimmer
A. Thompson	Carpenter
R. Hunt	A/B
J. O'Driscoll	A/B
J.D. Salter	A/B
E. Andsell	A/B
G.W. Woodcock	A/B
J.O. Neil	Sailor
W. Gibbon	Sailor
A. Milner	Sailor
G.L. Quinlan	Deck Boy
F. Dobie	Deck Boy

L.T. Weddell	O/Seaman
W.J. Fahey	Donkeyman, Stores and Greaser
F. Cureton	Greaser and Cleaner
C. Fletcher	Greaser and Cleaner
J. Shea	Cleaner
F. Doyle	Cleaner
	(Deserted ship at Liverpool. 20/4/1942)
F. McKenna	Cleaner
T. Murray	Cleaner
W. Morris	Cleaner
J. Ware	Chief Steward
A. D. Costa	Assistant Steward
W. Hobday	Assistant Steward
J. Williams	Assistant Steward
T.J. Jervis	Assistant Steward
C. Downes	Chief Ships Cook
W. Donaldson	Second Cook and Baker
C. Sturdy	Galley Boy
A. Dow	Stewards Boy

D.E.M.S. and Maritime Gunners

C. Andrews 3.Badge P.O.	Gunlayer
D.J. Wilkinson	Seaman Gunner
J.C.M. Wallis	Seaman Gunner
V. Panting	Seaman Gunner
G. Grassick	Seaman Gunner
W.T. Boldy	Seaman Gunner
J. Stead	Maritime Gunner
C. Smith	Maritime Gunner

U. 81

June 17th. 1943 . The Yoma torpedoed by the U.81.
The Commander was Kreig. Sank in Latitude 33
degrees 03 North 22 degres 04 East.
Note
A Mediterranean Convoy G.T.X.2. from Sfax
Tripolitania bound for Alexandria (I had been a
member of her Gun-crew at an earlier date.

Kptlt. Krieg, torpedoed the troopship S.S..Yoma full of French Troops in the Mediter-
ranean convoy G.T.X.2 . Very large loss of lives mostly Free French soldiers.

U.Boat 230

Convoy S.C. 121 Saturday March 6th. 1943 23-49hrs. EgyptianTorpedoed by "Siegman". Ship was 2,868 tons sank in 56degrees 25North. 37degrees 38 West

"Siegman" with his crew and Dockyard Dignitaries with his "U" Boat "U"230 attacked convoy S.C.121 March 6th. North Atlantic 1943

Sunday March 7th. 1943 15-30hrs. The Fort Lamy torpedoed by the "U" 527 The Commander was Uhlig. Sank in Latitude 58 degrees 30 North. 31 degrees 00.West

"U" 591

Kptl. Zetsche sank "Empire Impala" Sunday March 7th. 1943 at 09-06hrs she was 6,116 tons and sank in 58degrees North 15degrees West.
On Monday March 8th. 1943 at 16-21hrs. He torpedoed the "Vojvoda Putnik" in Latitude 58 degrees 42 North 31 degrees 25 West

"U" 526

Above. *The "U" 526 commanded by Möglich torpedoded and sank the "Guido" on Monday March 8th. 1943 08-55hrs Latitude 58degrees 08 North 32degrees 20 West.*

Below *The "U" 190 commanded by Kptlt Wintermeyer torpedoed and sank the "Empire Lakeland" on Monday March 8th. 1943 21-55hrs 1943 Latitude 58 degrees North 15 degrees West.*

"U".Boat 190

*Kptlt. Arth. Brünning "U"462 on Monday March 8th.
at 23-30 hrs torpedoed and sank the "Leadgate" in
Latitude 58degrees North 15degrees West"*

*Hans Gunther Lange Commander of the "U" 530 Attacked and sank the "Milos"
on March 9th. 1943. Latitude 58 degrees North 15 degrees West.*

"U".Boat 409

The "U" 409 torpedoed and sank the "Malantic" on Tuesday March 9th. 1943 at 21.28 hrs. and the "Rosewood" at 21.45hrs. Latitude 58degrees 37 North 22degrees 32 West.

Commander of the "U" 409 Massman Battle of the North Atlantic February and March 1943

"U".Boat 405

Kptlt. Hopman "U" 405 Wednesday March 10th. 1943 at 00-07hrs., he torpedoed the Commodore ship the "Bonneville" in Latitude 58degrees 45 North 21degrees 57 West. Very sadly the Commodore went down with his ship. He was one of our most experienced Commodores I had sailed with him in earlier convoys.

148

Commander Schetelig of the "U" 229

Wednesday, March 10th. 1943 the "Nailsea Court" was torpedoed by the "U" 229 at 00.05 hrs. Latitude 58degrees 45 North 21degrees 57 West Also the "Coulmore" torpedoed at 00.07 hrs. Latitude 58 degrees 48 North 22 degrees 00 West.

Kptlt. Krieg torpedoed the troopship S.S. "Yoma" full of French Troops in the Mediterranean. Convoy G.T.X.2. Bound for "Alexandria" 17.06 1943. Postition 33degrees 03 North 22degrees 04 East. Very large loss of lives mostly "Free French" soldiers.

Carl Emmermann Commander "U" Boat172 sank the Troopship "Orcades" Homeward from South Africa on the 10th. October 1942 at 10-28hrs., Position 31degrees 51 South 18degrees 30 East. I was seaman gunner on the M.V. Gascony at the time and the lookout spotted this lifeboat on the Port bow. It was number 17A we had just passed Tristan da Cuna. The master manouvered the ship alongside and we landed it on deck Strb., side of number 5 hold. We shared out the Horlicks tablets, Pemmican and condensed milk and carried No.17A all the way back to Liverpool returned to the P.&O.

"U".Boat 172

Captain F.J.Walker CB DSO

A most highly respected officer leaving his ship HMS Starling in Liverpool.
Captain Walker was a distinguished submarine hunter who it was said "could
smell a sub many miles and many fathoms beneath the surface".
He was responsible for the sinking of a number of German U boats.
Unfortunately the captain did not survive the war. On returning to his ship whilst
in Liverpool, he collapsed and died and was later buried at sea. His name will long
be remembered by those who served with and alongside him.

151

Chapter 9

ON LEAVE THEN BACK TO D.E.M.S. LIVERPOOL

When the children came in from school the first to arrive was Arthur, who was 10 years old. I was his hero and he was very pleased to see me and wanted to know if I had been in any fighting - and if I had killed any Japanese or Germans. Dorothy was next to arrive home, now aged 13, followed by 5 year old David. It was nice to see all the family again, especially my Uncle. He was anxious to know how things were going and to have news of our convoys.

We followed the familiar routine – tea at 5 o'clock then out to milk the cows. There were 16 and all had to be milked by hand. Electric milking machines were expensive and most small farmers could not afford them.

Over the evening meal my Uncle suggested that later we go out to his club and have a drink. I had to say I would rather have a hot bath and a good night's sleep as I had had very little rest on the passage from the States. I told him I would tell him all about my happenings over the next few days, but, as with most servicemen, you tend to kept things to oneself.

After enjoying the delicious home-cooked meal I sorted out the few presents I had managed to accumulate. Various kinds of chocolate for the children, Players cigarettes and pipe tobacco for my Uncle, and my Aunt was pleased that I had been able to bring home some ham, corned beef, fruit, Ceylon tea, rice, and, best of all, a pair of nylons.

I was glad to get to bed early and slept like a log for eleven hours. In the morning I was woken with a nice hot mug of tea and asked if I was up to joining the family for breakfast. I could smell the eggs and bacon frying! How good it was to be home!

I had lost touch with many friends, some of whom were away in the Services. I was sorry to hear that two schoolmates had been killed in action in the Royal Navy, and another two killed whilst serving in the Army. Over the next few days I visited relatives. It took some time to make up for the sleepless

152

days and nights, but after two weeks of good food and early nights, I began to feel a whole lot better.

My sister was a Sergeant Cook in the A.T.S. and stationed in Leicester. My brother John was Company Sergeant Major in the Royal Army Ordinance Corps and was somewhere preparing for the invasion of Sicily. However, to my surprise my Aunt had located them and they both managed to obtain a 72-hour pass so we could all spend some time together. Both their homes were fairly near the farm. This was our first meeting since Christmas 1941. On the Saturday evening we all went to my Uncle's Club and had a good drinking session. Neither he nor his farmer friends would let us buy any drinks. After a few games of darts and a singsong round the piano, I almost started to forget about the sad days at sea. Sunday was special. Somehow my Aunt had obtained a large joint of beef from the butcher. It was a happy time as we all sat round the huge kitchen table to enjoy a really splendid dinner. When Kathy and John left to report back to Barracks, that was to be the last time I would see them until the end of the war in the Far East. Our next get-together was Christmas 1945. My leave gradually came to an end and I was ready to join another ship. I had already decided to stay at sea when the war came to an end. I realised that I was not cut out to be a farmer. Farming is very hard work for very little wage.

I had to report back to D.E.M.S. Barracks Liverpool on 8th April 1943 and needed to get an early train from Chesterfield. My Uncle was doing his milk round so it was my Aunt who ordered the taxi and off the pair of us went to the station. When I boarded the train I think it was the first time I had seen my Aunt cry, but I told her I would be back again soon.

I arrived at Liverpool Lime Street at 11.30 a.m. and got sorted out before mid-day. Fortunately I did not have any Guard Detail to carry out so I was able to meet up with various Liverpool friends whom I had met whilst I was doing my Gunnery Course at H.M.S. Wellesley. It was nice to see them again, have a drink, enjoy fish and chips, and then back to Barracks.

I had five days in Liverpool and was then drafted down to Swansea.

The Barracks were full so I was billeted out with a very kind Welsh lady. I arrived there at about 7 p.m. in the pouring rain. I was quickly made to feel at home, given a comfortable room and in no time at all my landlady had prepared a lovely meal for me. Although it was a different bed, I had a good sleep and a good breakfast the following morning. I had to report to Barracks every day. As I was billeted out, once again I did not have to do Guard duties. I soon discovered that the Welsh Breweries make a good bitter, and I also tried their cider, or "Scrumpy".

On the 20th April 1943 a Messenger arrived to inform me that I would be collected at 09.30 hours the following day and would be signing on an English Tanker. So on the 21st April, having had 8 days of Welsh hospitality, I thanked the landlady for her excellent food, slung my two kit-bags and hammock on to the truck and we arrived at the docks and at my fifth war-time ship and second Tanker, the "Empire Flint".

M. V. Empire Flint

Chapter 10

M.V. EMPIRE FLINT

Builders: Swan-Hunter W & R, Wallsend on Tyne
Year: 1941
Gross Registered Tons: 8,129
Port of Registration: London. Off/Number: 51944

I carried one of my kit-bags aboard, and as one of the Gunners showed me to our accommodation, two of his mates carried my remaining kit-bag and hammock aboard.

The Gunlayer introduced me to the gun crew, then it was along to the Saloon to sign on. The Master was Captain H. Moore. He was efficient and proved it to all the crew in the way he handled the work of a saboteur whilst we were in the Port of Philadelphia. Then again later on during our passage back to the U.K. His decision at that time saved his ship and all the crew. Having seen one Tanker torpedoed in Convoy S.C. 121, those six days and nights of hell came flooding back to me. However, one had to be determined and I knew that I was going to survive – probably because of the blind faith in my St. Christopher's which never left the piece of string that was attached to my dog-tag.

"Good morning, Gunner, sign here". We all had to sign on the Ship's Articles for which we were awarded the princely sum of sixpence per day. (How kind of the ship owners!). The Master remarked "By your official number you have been in the Navy quite a long time". I told him it was 2 years and 2 months.

The Gunlayer was a Liverpudlian by the name of Jimmy Sadler. The Seaman Gunners were Claude Allen from Nottingham, Vic Oliver, Middlesex, Jock Campbell from Glasgow, Fred Bates from Leeds and Jack Stevens from Lancashire.

Being a new ship, built in 1941, the Gunners accommodation was good. Very roomy with two-tier bunks and accommodation for 10. The mess-room was separate. The Gunlayer had his own cabin and had his meals with the Bosun and Carpenter.

The armaments were one 4" B.L., one 12 pounder ack ack gun, and four 303 machine guns, smoke floats on the gun deck abaft the 4" shell racks.

The Second Mate, Mr. Jones, was the Gunnery Officer and we had gun drill before noon and also fire drill. After the gun drill, I went along and explained my frostbite problems to him. I showed him the type of painkiller I had been prescribed, and he assured me there would be no problems as every ship in the Merchant Navy carried them in the Medical Cabinet.

We sailed mid afternoon, carrying a lot of ballast to put us down a few feet and get the screw under water. When flying light, Tankers are worse than cargo ships as they do not have any top hamper in the way of Sampson Posts, derricks or jumboes. We sailed round to Liverpool and lay at anchor in the River Mersey. From there we sailed on 30th April 1943 in Convoy O.N. 181, but because of engine trouble we returned to the Clyde and dropped anchor on 2nd May. We were made sea-worthy and sailed on 6th May 1943 in Convoy O.N. 182. Destination was New York.

Extracted from Official A.D.M.'s:

Commodore: W.E.B. Magee in the Westland

Vice Commodore was the Master of the VOCO.

Local Escorts: Aquamarine (Armed Boarding Vessel) – known as "H.M. Trawler"

Paul Rykens (Trawler)

Southern Breeze and Helier II (Both A/S Whalers)

Ocean Escort Group: H.M.C.S. Ottawa. H/F D/F

H.M.S. Fishguard. H/F D/F

H.M.S. Dianthus, H.M.C.S. Arvina, H.M.C.S. Wetaskiwin, H.M.C.S. Rosthern, H.M.S.Banff, H/F D/F.

Support Group E.G.4: H.M.S. Faulknor, H.M.S. Onslaught, H.M.S. Impulsive (Joined a.m. 13th, left p.m. 14th).

Final Local Escort W14: H.M.C.S. Fennel, H.M.C.S. Nanaimo, H.M.C.S. Lachine, H.M.C.S.Montgomery.

Number of ships in Convoy: 57

Oilers: Thorshovdi, Chesapcake, Saintonge

Rescue Ships: Athelduchess

Rescue Tug: Storm King and St. Elstan.

A/S Trawler and Gothland. H/F, D/F/

Note The escorts for Convoy O.N. 182 had been changed from the Royal Navy to the Royal Canadian Navy. Therefore, some of our H.M.S. ships had the prefix H.M.C.S. I mention this to avoid any misunderstanding.

O.N. 182 sailed in "V" formation. Smoke trials were carried out during the voyage. The ocean escort, with the exception of H.M.S. Banff who sailed late, took over a.m. on the 7th May. The voyage was uneventful. A re-route was ordered by C. in C. Western Approaches on 9th May. To avoid another Convoy, on 10th May D/F bearings were sent out by a.m. on the 10th and at 19.39 hours on the 10th. E.G. 4 less Archer was told to proceed to reinforce O.N. 182. The weather was too bad for air cover on 12th May. On the 13th May, another re-route was ordered to avoid U-boats ahead. At this time E.G. 4 was in company. On 14th May, FONF suggested that ice fields made the route dangerous. It was accordingly amended to a.m. 15th May.

Dense fog was encountered on 16th May. At Westomp 38 ships were sighted but the remainder were widely scattered. W.14 had taken over escort by 21.00 hours on the 16th, and 26 ships were still missing. 53 ships had been collected by p.m. on the 18th, but at 17.15 hours on the 18th, the fog was dense and the convoy scattered. A/C co-operated in rounding up the M/Vs by a.m. on the 19th. New York ships arrived in on the 22nd May. The Vice Admiral arrived in on the 22nd. Vice Admiral Osborne and Commander Hodgson sailed in "Ottawa" to report on W.A.X. 03. **End of Note**

We arrived in New York on 22nd May 1943. Sixteen days of rolling and pitching across the North Atlantic. Some days were better than others, but generally the weather was kinder than I had experienced previously when I crossed the Atlantic East-bound in Convoy S.C. 121 in Force 10 with sleet, hail and snow.

The crew and gunners soon got to know each other. This Tanker had been handed over to the Athell Tanker Company. The Master, Mates, apprentices and Engineers, were all Athell-Line Company men. Most of the sailors and firemen were also Athell-Line seamen. Tanker men are a breed apart. They are purely and simply Tanker men and know their ships and how to maintain them, and will on no account, if they can avoid it, sign on cargo or passenger ships. The food served was of high quality, and curry was on the menu once a week. The Gunlayer was well liked and being a "Scouser" he had a good sense of humour. One of the Merchant Seamen, another "Scouser", carried his own guitar and, needless to say, was nicknamed Banjo. When the weather was favourable we would gather round and listen to him playing. His repertoire of Western songs was endless. Vic Oliver, one of the Seaman Gunners, had been trained as a singer and he, too, would often entertain us. There was a young seaman from Nottingham who talked endlessly about his girl friend back home who he was planning to get engaged to as soon as we returned to the U.K.

After swinging round the anchor in the River Hudson for 12 days, we sailed during the early hours of the 3rd June 1943 for Philadelphia.

As soon as we were alongside, no time was lost in getting coupled up and loading commenced with our cargo of Avgas which was destined for the invasion

of Sicily. Convoy V.G.S.Q. to Mediterranean. I was able to go ashore one day – the first time I had been ashore in America - and made a visit to a W.V.A. Centre. It was great to have some fresh milk and bread, and this was where I tasted coleslaw for the first time.

We were due to sail on the 4th June and meet up with the convoy for Sicily. However, disaster struck. When the Chief Engineer started the engines up, they started to check the Quadrant in the steering flat. It was quickly discovered that someone had poured about three buckets of sand into the gearing of the Quadrant, making us unseaworthy. The Master quickly got the local Police aboard, but whoever had sabotaged the ship was never found. It meant us going into dry-dock but there was not one large enough locally. The Master had to engage two large tugs to tow us round to New York. We arrived there on 8th June and we went straight into a huge floating dock "Todds Dry Dock Brooklyn". Fortunately, we were allowed into this floating dry dock fully laden because America was free of air raids.

We were immediately inundated with F.B.I. Officers and also Royal Naval Officers. Everyone was interviewed individually by both branches. No one was allowed ashore while the questioning was in progress. We had to be content to just gaze at the New York skyline. After four days the F.B.I. and Royal Navy Officers cleared the ship for shore leave and left us.

What happened next came as a surprise to my shipmates who had never been ashore in America. We were all informed that before we were allowed ashore we would have to undergo what was known as a "short arm inspection". This did not take very long as four Doctors came aboard. This was a strict regulation to prevent any form of venereal disease entering the country.

After this delay some American currency was brought aboard. We worked out how much money we could draw and it proved to be just about sufficient for our needs. Unfortunately, half the gunners had to stay on board for fire-watch so it was three ashore and three on board. I went ashore on the 13th with Vic Oliver and Claude Allen. Vic had been to New York before so on his instructions we made a beeline for the famous Stage Door Canteen. Claude and I were overwhelmed by its size. There were servicemen of every nationality, though, of course, predominantly Americans. There was no beer or alcohol but as much fresh milk as we could drink and Coca-Cola. Also a really good Help-Yourself delicatessen counter where we could get ice cream. We took our time and had an excellent meal.

We then set off to do a little sightseeing around Times Square. The first thing we wanted to do was to buy some Nylon stockings while we still had some American dollars. We all bought four pairs to take back to England. We then visited Jack Dempsey's Bar. He happened to be there at the time and that made it a special time for us. You could buy a giant rump steak at the bar, but having had one good meal, we felt we couldn't do justice to another!

We had been given complimentary tickets at the Stage Door Canteen to attend a film show at the Paramount Theatre on Broadway. It was a good film and a splendid show and I remember we saw the famous Andrew Sisters. We were much impressed with the theatre – by far the largest one any of us had seen. One thing I particularly remember was that during the interval I went out to the Gents and on returning to my seat I discovered, to my horror, that I had left my parcel of nylons behind and I knew I did not have enough dollars to buy more. I raced back and to my relief they were still there!

Vic had thought up a plan to save money. After the free show at the Paramount Theatre, we would go back again to the Stage Door Canteen for a meal before getting the launch back to the ship. The Canteen was much busier than it had been on our first visit but we still had a good meal and were given some free cigarettes.

We then got the launch and were back aboard our ship before mid-night.

The following day, 14th June, was our day aboard for fire watch duties, etc.

Note from A.D.M. 199/578

We weighed anchor during the early hours of 15th June and proceeded to Halifax to join Convoy H.X. 244. (Note sailing time was 04.00 hours)

The Commodore was Sir Raymond Fitzmaurice R.N.R. His ship was The Empire Bunting. The Vice Commodore was Commodore Meek, R.N.R. His ship was the Eskbank. This was a very big convoy, 78 ships sailed from New York, 18 ships sailed from Halifax, to join Convoy H.X. 244, making a total of 93 ships. Seven ships got lost in the dense fog off and after Halifax. They returned to Halifax or St. Johns Newfoundland, leaving 86 ships in the Convoy. The Commodore ship was the lead ship of the 7th column.

The Vice Commodore ship was the lead ship of the 10th column. Empire Flint was the 4th ship of the third column. There were 7 ships in our column, and each one was loaded with petrol, fuel-oil, Avgas, Avgas and diesel, and petrol products.It made me shudder, but there are no back doors at sea.

This was a mighty armada of ships. Total of 12 columns. 11 columns had 7 ships and the 8th column had 1 only, making a total of 78 cargo ships and tankers. The Commodore's instructions were that the distance between columns was to be maintained at 1,000 yards. The distance between ships in columns to be maintained at 500 yards. The speed was to be 9 knots.

Our escorts from New York
H.M.S. Chelsea "Senior Officer"
H.M.S. Shawingam
H.M.S. Barrie
H.M.S. Oliesenel
All the above left at 13.50 hours on 20th June.

Our escorts from Halifax
H.M.S. Buxton "Senior Officer"
H.M.S. Buctauche
H.M.S. Nipigon
All the above left at 18.15 hours on 19th June.

Lat. 44 degrees 43' North.   Long. 51 degrees 09' West

Joined 13.50 hours on 20th June
H.M.S. Burnham "Senior Officer Ocean Escort"
H.M.S. Lalmalmaie
H.M.S. Barle
H.M.S. Mayflower
H.M.S. Picton
H.M.S. Bittersweet
H.M.S. Skeena

Joined 12.15 hours 23rd June

H.M.S. Lulworth) 40th Group
H.M.S. Bideford)

H.M.S. Hastings) Support Group
H.M.S. Waverley)
Support Group left 14.20 hours June 26th.   Remaining escorts left off
Oversay June 29th.

H.X. 244

Sailed from New York   75 ships

Sailed from Halifax   <u>18 ships</u>   Total: 93 ships

7 ships lost Convoy in fog and returned to Halifax or St.John

14 fast ships were detached to various destinations 14.20 hours June 26th

4 11 knot ships were detached at 20.15 hrs. June 28th to catch the tide for Liverpool

At 04.00 hours 9 ships detached

For Loch Ewe   Total: 34 ships = 59 ships remaining

At 05.00 June 29th, the Belfast, Clyde and Mersey ships were ordered to proceed to their destinations and all have arrived safely, which makes a total of 86 ships that arrived safely in the U.K.

During the fog and very bad visibility that we were experiencing off Iceland, the Master made a decision to slip the Convoy and we set a course for the Arctic Circle 66 degrees 33' North and beyond. We encountered giant icebergs – my first experience of them. The size of some of them was mind boggling and I regret that I did not have a camera. The only other ship that we encountered in those icy wastes was one Naval vessel in the distance on our Port Bow which was having firing practice at one of the icebergs. The vessel looked very much like a Corvette to me. The Officer on watch exchanged Morse signals with her.

I have vivid recollections of the extreme cold. On watch we had plenty of warm clothing and wore extra thick "John Ells", extra vests and thick sea-boot stockings, a duffel coat, Balaclava and fur-lined gloves (Naval issue). The cold weather was once again playing havoc with my knees and legs. The pain killing tablets that the Second Mate provided helped to alleviate some of the pain. The Master ordered the Chief Steward to give all hands a tot of run on four consecutive days. This was a very kind gesture which everyone really appreciated. Sailing in these conditions was for most of us an unforgettable experience and although I spent 22 years at sea after the war, I'm glad to say I never had to experience a sea crossing to compare with it.

Having successfully dodged any lurking U-boats by taking us beyond the Arctic Circle, the Master hauled her round and we made Oversay on the 29th June 1943.   Oversay (or Orsay) on the extreme west coast of Scotland, is a small lighthouse on the Isle of Islay.   There we starboard the helm and enter the North Channel, round Malin Head and into the North Channel where we parted company with the ships bound for Glasgow. Down past the Isle of Man where the Liverpool-bound ships left us, proceeding on into St. George's Channel, rounding Milford Haven and Pembroke and had to anchor off Swansea for a few days.

Before we went alongside, all the ammunition was stowed away in the magazine and we had all got our bags packed ready to sign off. However, the D.E.M.S. Officer informed us that it would be Monday before we would be collected to proceed home on leave.

The sad part is that when I went ashore on the Saturday, during my absence someone had forced the lock on my small case and stolen the nylon stockings I had bought in New York. We eventually signed off on the 16th July, making this a short trip of 2 months and 15 days.

Before transport arrived, I went along and shook hands with the Master and Mates, then said farewell to all the crew who had been good mates. Most of them were going on leave, then signing on again as they were "Tankermen". The Chef made a bigger than normal breakfast, as is usual on a "signing off" day. I had a hurried bowl of thick porridge (into which I stirred what was left of my tin of condensed milk), a piece of haddock, and 2 eggs and bacon to make an extra large "butty".

The R.N. Transport arrived at 09.30 hours. Our gear was already on the wharf. Before I went down the gangway I gave this beautiful Tanker a slap on the fish-plate and said "thank you ship for getting me home safely". When we arrived at the D.E.M.S. Barracks we were told to leave our gear aboard the truck and go and collect our leave money and railway passes, then to the local station for a train home. When I collected my pay and leave allowance, I discovered I had been awarded 28 days leave. I was then to report to D.E.M.S. Glasgow on 13th August 1943. Although I had only been away on a short voyage, the D.E.M.S. pool of trained Gunners was being increased all the time, enabling longer leaves.

I said goodbye and good luck to the other Gunners and I never saw them again during the war. However, when I went back to sea after the war who should I meet on my first ship (the "Paraguay") but the Gunlayer Jimmy Sadler – now a Boss Stevadore.

The good news which I received from the Lt. Commander, D.E.M.S., Swansea, was that I had been recommended to go for a Gunlayers Course at Leith. This must have been on the recommendation of Captain H. Moore of Empire Flint and the Gunlayer.

NOTE

Empire Flint was managed by the Athell-Line. She survived the war and in 1945 was re-named the "Athelstane".

In 1952 she was sold and re-named "Oakley".

In 1961 the owner was recorded as Torvald-Klaveness (Norway). She was broken up for scrap in Hamburg 1961

Names of Master, Officers, Crew and Gunners of
M.V. "Empire Flint"

H. Moore	Master
R.E. Kibble	Chief Officer
H.L. Jones	Second Officer
R.G. Gray	Third Officer
G. Taylor	Chief Engineer
H.S. Bowan	Second Engineer
S. Fisk	Third Engineer
D.A. Murray	Fourth Engineer
J. Smith	Fifth Engineer
J. Morley	Sixth Engineer
J. Wilson	First Radio Officer
M. Kerr	Second Radio Officer
E. Sterling	Third Radio Officer
I. Portious	Apprentice

M.P. Shillito	Apprentice
W.R. Morton	Apprentice
J.B. Kirkham	Apprentice
J. Cowley	Carpenter
H.J. Jones	Bosun
R. Hugill	A/B
E. Branagan	A/B
W. Carine	A/B
J.C. White	A/B
J. Manley	A/B
F.L. James	A/B
V. Draper	A/B
P. Saunders	E.D.H.
E. Breden	E.D.H.
F. Meers	E.D.H.
R. Baker	E.D.H.
R. Southall	O/S
D. Robinson	O/S
M. Humphries	Donkeyman
W. Vaughan	Donkeyman/Greaser
W. Howard	Greaser
F. McDaid	Greaser
D. Law	Fireman/Wiper
A.H. Lamb	Fireman/Wiper
T.W. Wright	Fireman/Wiper
H.J. Chigner	Fireman/Wiper
J. Roberts	Fireman/Wiper

(Deserted ship – New York, 6th June 1943)

E. Clarke	Chief Steward
C. Roberts	Second Steward
C.S. Hill	M.R. Steward
J. Jones	M.R. Boy

166

K. Merrifield	Cabin Boy
W. Somerville	Ship's Cook
G.W. Marsh	Second Cook
R.L. Shaw	Galley Boy

D.E.M.S. Gunners (Note: No Maritime Gunners)

J.T. Sadler	P/O Gunlayer
C. Campbell	A/B Seaman Gunner
C.A. Allen	A/B Seaman Gunner
G. Grassick	A/B Seaman Gunner
V. Oliver	A/B Seaman Gunner
F. Bates	A/B Seaman Gunner
J. Stevens	A/B Seaman Gunner

Chapter 11

FROM "EMPIRE FLINT" TO HOME

At Sheffield Station I had to change trains and board the local for Chesterfield. It was just over half an hour's run. On arrival I was lucky to find a taxi. As any ex-sailor will agree, going on leave and carrying both kit bags and hammock, plus a small suitcase, is a bit of a problem. I had signed off my ship in Swansea and was instructed to report to D.E.M.S., Glasgow, on 13th August – hence I had all my gear with me.

I don't recall what time I arrived home but the taxi took me through the gates and down the 80 yards round to the back of the house. Both my Aunt and Uncle were seated on the old stone Cheese Press having a mug of tea. I had only been away for a short while so after an exchange of "great to see you again" the first question was "How much leave have you got this time?" They were surprised when I told them 28 days. I explained that this was because there were now more trained gunners in the D.E.M.S. Pool.

My Aunt's children were soon home from school and there was a lot of questions and talking to be done. I enjoyed a lovely home cooked meal. This is always much appreciated, particularly by servicemen on leave. I must say, however, that the Chief Steward and Cook on the "Empire Flint" made sure that we were served really good food. This is how the Company kept their crews. Good Masters and Officers, and good food, and you have a contented crew!

I knew what was going on in the minds of the children. "Has George brought us any chocolate". I had saved most of my sweet ration, including a few tins of chocolate from the Stage Door Canteen, so there was plenty to go round. I was sorry to tell my Aunt that I did not have any nylon stockings for her as they had been stolen. Someone had also stolen my cigarettes and tobacco. They were packed in my kit bag when I left the ship and can only have been stolen during the time my kit bags were in the Guards Van on the train. Fortunately nothing else was taken. I said I would go into Chesterfield the following day and get new locks for my kit bag!

My Uncle finally finished his jobs in the farmyard – the hand milking, then turning the cows out into the fields, etc. During the summer the cows sleep out at night in the field, as do the horses. We spent several hours talking and catching up with the news.

I didn't experience the extreme tiredness on this leave as I did after convoy S.C. 121. My heartfelt thanks go out to the Master of the "Empire Flint" in getting his ship away from the U-boat packs by taking us up and over the Arctic Circle.

In the evening I enjoyed a traditional Northern supper. There was homemade bread, cheese and pickled onions and a glass of milk. Milk was always served in the summer and cocoa in the winter. I had a hot bath and then slept like a log until 6.30 a.m. when I was awoken by the dog bringing the cows in to be milked. His loud barking soon made me decide to get up!

I took my Aunt her early morning tea and very soon she had a huge breakfast prepared and had got the children off to school. I got myself smartened up and was ready to start my round of visits to friends and relatives, which I knew would occupy quite a few days. The weather was kind to me and it stayed dry and sunny for the whole of my leave.

After two weeks my supply of painkillers began to get low and I went along to see our family doctor. His surgery was closed but he asked me in and gave me some more painkilling tablets. He then went and got some tea for us both. I soon realized he was anxious to hear about the war at sea and our convoy system. I told him about Convoy SC 121 and that we had lost many good seamen. We had a long chat and on leaving I gave him a packet of American cigarettes – Lucky Strike.

I had one more call to make - another Aunt - and then made my way home. I noticed that there were quite a number of American servicemen wherever I went. This, of course, was the build up in preparation for the invasion of Europe. I mentioned this to my Uncle and he took delight in telling me of some local scandal. A certain house at the end of the village that was used as a meeting place for American soldiers, mostly at night when they were off duty. In other words, he said, the local brothel!

I saw my father who worked at Chesterfield Tube Works. He told me that he and his work mates were machining the special noses for the Tall Boys. The large 12-ton bombs that were being used to obliterate the U-boat pens at Hamburg and elsewhere.

After the war I was A/B on a Blue Funnel ship that was being repaired and dry docking at Hamburg. One afternoon a party of us went to look at the state of the U-boat pens. It had been left exactly as our Lancaster Bombers had left it – a complete shambles. Parts of the 30 or 40 foot thick roof had just simply caved in under the pressure of the intensive bombing raids and had fallen across many of the U-boats. I felt proud of the fact that my father had helped to disable this construction.

My leave appeared to flash by quickly. My sister had managed to get a 48-hour pass from her Barracks in Leicester. She now had the rank of Sergeant Cookery Instructor. (She met an Army Sergeant also stationed there to whom she married when the war in Europe ended.)

My brother could not join us on this occasion as he took part in the invasion of Sicily (Operation Husky) on July 10th 1943. This was when the Allies landed General Montgomery with his Eighth Army, and General (Blood and Guts) Patton and the United States Seventh Army. On the first day approximately 150,000 troops landed. The final total was about 478,000, of which 250,000 were British and 228,000 were American. The Naval operations were conducted by Admiral Sir Andrew Cunningham. By the morning of 17th August 1943, the last German soldier had been flung out of Sicily. Sir Winston Churchill's early decision was to attack and take Sicily, then on into Italy "the soft underbelly of Europe". This proved to be right and gained the Allies a hard-earned victory. My brother fought all the way across Italy and into Germany. He told me of one particular incident where a large number of Italian soldiers waved the white flag of surrender amid rumours that the end of the war was in sight, and that Mussolini himself was about to surrender. The interesting part was that the Italian solders had with them three huge caravans full of well-dressed prostitutes, and also dozens of cases of wine. These were duly shared out – the wine that is!

Shortly after my brother's best mate had been killed when a barrage of shells were loosed upon them, he charged into action and killed over 60 enemy soldiers. He was awarded the Mentioned in Dispatches Medal.

My leave came to an end and it was soon time to journey to D.E.M.S. Barracks, Glasgow. I made my farewells and got an early train heading North. I knew it was going to be a long haul – a distance of 435 miles. But I had plenty of cigarettes and my Aunt had given me a good supply of bacon sandwiches and hard boiled eggs. I think the train stopped at every station and as we passed through I noticed that the emphasis was on troop movement. It suddenly dawned on me that the Clyde was a No. 1 port "Gourock" for the movement of troopships. I had vivid recollections of the very large convoy that my ship "M.V. Pardo" sailed in. 12th January 1942 Convoy W.S. 15 consisting of sixteen troopships bound for Singapore. Two of the soldiers sharing the compartment were going all the way to Glasgow. They were both in the R.A.M.C. and had survived Dunkirk, so they must have been very proud of their Sargeant's stripes. I shared my sandwiches and eggs with them and it was late in the afternoon when we pulled into St. Enochs Station, Glasgow.

I said farewell to the two R.A.M.C. Medics and retrieved my hammock and kit bags from the Guards Van. I then reported to the Regulating Petty Officer who, in turn, quickly organised transport for me to the D.E.M.S. Barracks, which was a ten-minute drive away. I found I was to be housed in a comfortable room that had twelve hospital type beds, and also a locker. I did not have long to wait for an evening meal. Then a good hot shower and some sleep. As usual, the train journey had made me tired.

I rose early on the 14th and went to see the Medical Officer at 09.30 hours. My legs and knees were subjected to a rigorous examination. The Lieutenant Commander wanted to know the origin of my problem so I put my mind back to February and March of 1943 and Convoy S.C. 121. The terrible weather conditions that prevailed at the time and my encounter with the giant icebergs during my time aboard the "Empire Flint".

The examination over, I was informed that I had to put my kit into storage, just keep my shaving gear, etc. then get transport to the Southern General Hospital. I was admitted to the Southern General about mid-day. The Matron allocated me to a bed and I discovered that there was a Merchant Seaman in the next bed to me. He was a real old Shellback, had been at sea since 1930 and had also been torpedoed. I had two nurses allocated to me, Nurse Ross and Nurse Donaldson, and they were both super efficient and looked after me well. They were also practical jokers. There was some form or regulation about smoking, but I remember we were allowed to smoke at certain times.

Part of my treatment in hospital was to have very hot baths four times a day. The bath was larger than an ordinary one and was more than half filled with very hot water. Something was added to the water and whatever it was helped the nagging pain that I had been enduring since February to disappear. When I had dried myself off, both legs were then massaged by one of the nurses.

I was discharged the first week in October and went back to D.E.M.S. Barracks. I had to wait for the Gunlayer's Course at D.E.M.S. Leith to finish and I was logged in for the next one. Because I had been discharged from hospital, I was excused Guard Duty. I was pleased to be included in a local Gunnery Course and practice shoot with the two types of guns they were now mounting on Merchant Ships. One was a 4" dual purpose gun with a shield, using fixed ammunition, both for submarines or aircraft. To us D.E.M.S. Gunners, this was a super gun - "Dual Purpose". The other one was the Oerlikon 20mm gun for defence against air attack. The magazine held sixty rounds. This was sheer magic compared with the obsolete World War I guns that had been taken out of mothball depots and hastily bolted aboard our proud old Merchant ships at the beginning of the war.

I managed to get up into the centre of Glasgow, which was teeming with American servicemen. My daily intake of tablets had been stopped so it was safe to drink a pint of their excellent Scotch Bitter. I struck up a conversation with three American soldiers from Brooklyn and when I told them about my visit to the Stage door Canteen and Paramount theatre, they would not let me buy a round of beer. Of course, there was no comparison between servicemen's rates of pay in England and U.S

The time quickly came round for me to get a train across to Leith where I arrived on 9th October 1943. The Gunnery School was aboard an old World War I sloop, "H.M.S. Claverhouse", moored in Leith Docks. I don't remember the number of Seaman Gunners in the class, but we all shared a very spacious mess deck and our hammocks were used. The ship was under the Command of Commander Simpson, Royal Navy. A retired World War I Commander who was held in high esteem.

The Gunlayer's Course proved to be very interesting and I had good shipmates. Most of them had been at sea as long as I had, nearly three years, so we had quite a lot of war stories to exchange. We had two very good Royal Navy Gunnery Instructors, both pre-war and also Chief Petty Officers. We were brought right up-to-date with all the latest in defensive armaments, including the two I had already done a course on at Glasgow, and I still had the Instruction Manual on both of them. I was pleased to do the course on the 6" gun, as this was not included in the course at H.M.S. Wellesley. Much later on, whilst serving in the Far East, I served on a Troop ship which was equipped with six 6" guns.

When the afternoon session was over and we had finished our evening meal, we used to do a bit of "cramming". We would sling our hammocks, climb aboard and get stuck into the various Instruction Manuals. If our money would allow it, one of us would go to the local Fish and Chip shop. When Commander Simpson was staying aboard he would always ask whoever went to also bring him back fish and chips.

There was an efficient tram service to Edinburgh which took us all the way up Princes Street. I liked to go there on a Saturday or Sunday and mingle with the crowd.

The Course was soon over and all the class became fully fledged A/B Gunlayers, which increased our pay by sixpence a day. Most of us had a drink at a local dockside pub as a way of celebration. Then for me it was another train journey Westbound to Glasgow and I reported back again on the 8th November.

I was informed that I was being drafted to a ship bound for Murmansk, Russia. When I went before the Medical Officer he immediately put a stop to it. He told me that as I had already done six North Atlantic crossings he was going to get me drafted to a ship that would take me into warmer climates. It did not take long as on 9th November I got drafted to the Blue Funnel ship "M.V. Orestes".

M.V. Orestes

Chapter 12

M.V. ORESTES

M.V. Orestes was built by Workman Clark & Co. Belfast for the Ocean
Steam Ship Company in 1926.
Gross tonnage: 7,845
Port of Registry: Liverpool
Off/Number: 70421

In May 1942 M.V.Orestes was attacked by Japanese aircraft off Madras but
escaped serious damage.

June 9th 1942. She was attacked by three Japanese submarines that had sur-
faced off Sydney Heads and suffered shrapnel holes in the funnel but again
escaped serious damage.

She also took part in the invasion of North Africa and survived the war.

In 1963 M.V. Orestes was sold in August to Nichimen & Co. Ltd., Osaka,
Japan, for £84,500 for scrap and broken up at Mihara.

This ship was the first of her class to be fitted with electric-cargo winches. An
earlier "Orestes" opened up the first direct cargo service between the U.K. and
Australia in 1901.

On 9th November 1943 I was drafted to the Blue Funnel Ship M.V. Orestes.
She was berthed at the King George V Docks and it was a long drive out to
her. I was to learn in later years that the dock was owned by Blue Funnel, and
I was to dock there many times after the war when I was A/B with the Com-
pany.

Once on board I was shown my accommodation. It was a cabin for two,
which I shared with the Petty Officer Gunlayer. Three Badge – the same as
Jock Andrews of the "Gascony". The remaining Gunners had a large cabin
that had two-tier bunks and a table in the centre. The mess room was adjacent
to the accommodation. It was rather cramped and there was only just suffi-
cient room for all twelve gunners at the mess room table – six either side. There
was a steam boiler to provide hot water for tea and coffee, but storage space

was very limited. Hardly any space to keep dry goods, such as bread, butter and jam, although we did get the Chippy to utilise a corner that had been over-looked when the accommodation was built. The showers and toilets were situated up on the gun deck abaft the 4" gun and the deck had been strength-ened to mount the 12 pounder ack ack gun.

Altogether there was a total of 13 D.E.M.S. and Maritime Ack Ack Gunners. The Gunnery Officer and Second Mate was Mr. Crake.

The Second Mate came along to inform me to report to the Saloon at 11.00 hrs as a Shipping Master was coming aboard to sign on crew members. I duly went along to sign on for my sixpence per day, and the Master, Captain Purkis, welcomed me aboard. I quickly got acquainted with the other Gunners and got my gear sorted out. My cabin was fairly spacious and the P.O. I shared it with was a likeable character.

My first taste of Blue Funnel food was the mid-day meal that was brought along from the Galley. The food was excellent and, apart from the Dutch Tanker, "Orestes" was the best "feeder" I had served on. The cooks were both Chi-nese and I had my first introduction to chicken-chow-mien which was usually served twice a week. Most gunners and sailors always went back for "sec-onds", much to the delight of the cooks.

After dinner Charlie showed me all the armaments for the defence of the ship. This consisted of one World War I 4" B.L. situated on the raised poop deck. Abaft of the 4" B.L. and situated above the gunners showers and toilets was a 12 pounder ack ack gun, and we also had one mounted for'ard on the Fore-castle Head, cleverly mounted over the anchor cable with the magazine below in the forepeak. There was a 303 machine gun on each wing of the Bridge and one on either side of the boat deck.

On top of the radio shack, two F.A.M.S. were mounted. She also carried the normal amount of smoke floats at the after end of the gun deck behind the shell racks. Also four depth charges attached to mountings round the stern with a quick-release fitting. All they required was the setting for depth to be adjusted. The day after I joined we had gun drill at 10.00 hours. The Second Mate was the Gunnery Officer. I was No.2 on the 4" B.L. and in case of air attack I was in charge of the 12 pounder on the Forecastle Head. The Chief Mate was in charge of the Fire Party.

We sailed under cover of darkness on 11th November 1943 and watches were set four on and eight off. Having a good turn of speed we headed out into the North Atlantic on our own. We were a light ship so "Orestes" soon started to perform. She was a very good ship and I quickly got familiar with the way she tackled the sea.

Our destination was to be St. John's, New Brunswick, to load war supplies for Australia, where American troops were being trained and assembled for the assault on Japan. We had an uneventful passage across to St. John's but there had been a change in the weather, force eight and snowing all the time. There had been very heavy snow at St. John's and it stayed with us all the time while loading was in progress.

As soon as we had berthed and got the shells and small arms ammunition away, the Second Mate came long and told Charlie that a Fire Watch had to be maintained which called for two gunners to patrol the vicinity of the magazines – one Navy and one Army gunner on for four hours.

We got ashore at the first opportunity to have a look around and we found a friendly response from the Canadian people. However, we discovered that they had strict liquor laws and to obtain spirits or beer the locals and visiting seamen had to go to a Government Department and be issued with a ration book. One of the Maritime Gunners (Harry Smith, a Yorkshireman) got one and so did Charlie the P.O.

To our surprise we had a visit from a local group who ran the Seamen's Union to inform us that they were going to invite us all to an early Christmas Dinner at the Mission. The Second Mate said that he would get two of the crew to do the Fire Watch. They gave us the date and we all went along, except the P.O. and Bosun who wanted to get their liquor allocation. Twelve of us turned up and there were enough young ladies to go round! It was a real Christmas dinner, with turkey and all the trimmings, Christmas pudding and beer for everyone. I walked a young Canadian girl home and enjoyed a mug of coffee with her and her father. He was really hospitable and it was a most pleasant evening.The following day we sailed early for New York and watches were again set fours hours on eight hours off, the weather was still unsettled and snowing. It was very cold so it was back into duffel coats and deep sea boot stockings once again. U boats were still operating right up to the west coast of Canada and America

As soon as we tied up at our berth in New York, fire watches were set and we drew lots for going ashore. We had the same Customs routine that I had experienced on the Tanker "Empire Flint". Four of us then went ashore and we made straight for the Stage Door Canteen. Only Stan, the Maritime Gunner, and myself had been to New York before. Our companions were Albert (who we had to call Eddie) Hawkins, and young Tommy Sutton, who was from Birmingham and on his first trip to sea as seaman gunner. As we made our way out of the dock area and up to the City he found it hard to believe the sight of cars and taxis speeding by and the mass of coloured lights and brilliantly lit advertisement hoardings – all so different from what we had left back home. We enjoyed a splendid meal at the Stage Door Canteen which was all free and much appreciated. We were each given a ticket to the Paramount Theatre on Broadway and to our delight Frank Sinatra was appearing. The front rows of the theatre were jammed full of young girls - "Bobby Soxers" as they were then known.

After the theatre we visited Jack Dempsey's Bar, but as we were all short of dollars we then went back to the Stage Door Canteen before returning to the ship.

Loading was in progress when we got back and we learned that the dockers would be working round the clock to get her down to her marks. The great advantage was, of course, that there were no blackouts and no air raids.

It was an impressive sight – cargo coming to the docks twenty-four hours a day, stacked on the wharf and inside the warehouses. A continual stream of trains and trucks. There were massive wooden crates, tanks, lorries, jeeps and aircraft. Ours was all bound for Australia where the American and Canadian troops were being trained for the invasion of Japan.

After the Japanese bombed Pearl Harbour ("the Day of Infamy") a Japanese Admiral was purported to have remarked "We have now awakened a sleeping giant". By what we were witnessing at the docks they had indeed awakened a sleeping giant.

We were quickly down to our marks, including deck cargo which was in wooden crates and all lashed and secured by shore riggers. We sailed on our own, down through the Caribbean and on into Panama. This was my first trip through the Panama Canal and it was quite awe-inspiring. The three huge locks at the Atlantic side were called the Gatun Locks. Each one lifted us up to a height of 60 feet, the ship being held in a vice-like grip by four huge 3" wires, two for'ard and two aft, the slack being taken up by four huge winches (mules as the Americans called them). After the first 60 feet we were then manoeuvred into No.2 lock and the huge stern gates locked us in to be pumped the remaining 60 feet into the third and final lock. The wire ropes were then cast off and we were free to proceed under our own power through the lakes. On reflection I well remember what a magnificent sight it was looking down on to the Atlantic Ocean from a height of 180 feet.

The Canal Zone was controlled by the American military who had invested millions of dollars into the project to connect two mighty oceans together. This saved the Ship owners a substantial amount of money by cutting out the long and dreary haul round Cape Horn.

We made steady progress through the Lakes to Balboa and on to the locks on the Pacific side, the "Miraflore Locks". This was another breathtaking sight. We were now looking down and over the Pacific Ocean. The procedure was the same but this time the ship was lowered by three 60 foot drops, a total of 180 feet, to get us into the Pacific Ocean. As soon as the Pilot disembarked we were on our way. Gun watches were set and the ship was once again back to normal routine. Very soon the shoreline and ships had disappeared from view and all one could see was miles and miles of sea. The vastness of the mighty Pacific Ocean where trade routes cut a few known narrow canals across wastes of water where no keel has ever been.

Our course was set for Australia. We all knew that we were going to Sydney as the Americans had stencilled it all over the packing cases. The weather was really hot and we took advantage of it and did a lot of sunbathing. The sun was of benefit to my legs and knees and pain-killing tablets became a thing of the past, which was a great relief.

New Year's Day 1944 was approaching and the Master, Captain Purvis, did a noble thing and we went slightly off course and anchored in the Harbour off Hawaii. In the early hours of January 1st the Second Mate came along and informed the P.O. that the Master had made this decision to enable us all to have New Year's Day dinner together. No watches were kept as we were quite safe, and we would up anchor at 16.00 hours. The two Chinese cooks prepared a really wonderful meal for us, which consisted of roast pork and Christmas pudding. The gunners and crew all received a bottle of beer each. The Master was a real gentleman!

To reminisce I have vivid recollections of being in dry dock for two weeks in Kobe, Japan, after the war when our ship was having part of the hull re-riveted. It was Christmas Day and we had been ashore for a quick drink. We met up with the crew of a Tramp ship (I will not repeat the name). The Chief Steward and cook had sold all the food and for Christmas dinner the crew had cold corned beef and potatoes. Our Chef took pity on them and gave all eight of the crew a good dinner, compliments of Blue Funnel.

We upped anchor at 16.00 hours and were once again heading for Sydney. The weather remained very hot and the sea stayed glassy. We experienced the occasional squally shower but the sea was never rough, just one long low swell. "Orestes" was a very good ship at sea; she developed a slow steady roll with hardly any pitching at all. We arrived at Sydney Heads in the early hours of the morning, watches were broken and we got all the shells stowed away and covered up the 4" 12 pounders and the machine guns.

The D.E.M.S. and Maritime Officers were aboard soon after breakfast. They made a quick inspection of the defence system and much to every-one's delight there was no mention of any refresher courses. All we had to do was sort ourselves out and make a roster for the normal fire and magazine watches, just two aboard at all times. I was eager to get ashore as I had heard so many stories about this great country. When I did go ashore I was impressed with the famous Circular Quay where there was a never-ending arrival and departure of trams – much the same as our UK ones. There were a lot of fish stalls situated near to the pubs and local bars that sold prawns. The local practice was to buy a bag of these very large and delicious prawns and then go into the nearest bar and have a schooner of Australian beer or lager that was served ice cold. This was the first Australian habit that I gladly adopted. There was an abundance of cheap fresh fruit, bananas, oranges, apples, grapes and pineapples. After our cold beer we decided on a tour of the shops and stores. The problem was making our money spin out. The extra pay I received for my Gunlayer's badge had bumped my weekly pay up a little, and on 4th February 1944 I had completed my three years service. This entitled me to wear one good conduct badge and there was another slight adjustment to my pay, but this did not make a great deal of difference.

We were three weeks discharging all the Canadian and American military cargo. The Australian dockers were hard workers. As soon as the sailors had got the holds cleaned of broken dunnage and cargo mats we commenced loading for New York. "Orestes" was fitted with refrigeration holds and these were filled with frozen lamb. The dockers had a perfect way of loading them so as to keep a level flooring - belly to belly and back to back and they stowed them very quickly. They also loaded boxes of butter and hundreds of large tins of ham. This cargo would eventually arrive in England via New York.

This mixed cargo I could not name exactly, as some of my wartime diaries went missing when my suitcase was stolen on a passage from New Zealand to the UK in 1964. My sextant and uniforms were also in the case. The day we sailed from Sydney to New York one of the Maritime Gunners, Harry Smith, a Yorkshire man, got drunk and set fire to himself. He had fallen asleep and his cigarette smouldered through his thick army shirt. Fortunately, one of the Gunners raised the alarm and doused the fire with buckets of water or the accommodation could have gone up in smoke. We got the Ship's Doctor along who gave Harry an injection to kill the pain as he was badly burnt from his neck down to his navel. It was the worst case of burns I have ever witnessed. He was unable to stand his watch until a few days before we arrived back in New York, so we had a passenger on our hands for three weeks!

We had a reasonably calm passage all the way from **Sydney to** New York. The vastness of the Pacific Ocean favoured us once again. Just the occasional heavy squall to cool the decks down. We had an abundance of very hot weather enabling me to stretch out as often as possible to get some sun on my legs.

Arriving in New York we had no delay in getting a berth and the holds were quickly opened up. The sailors were very professional, most of them being Blue Funnel men. All derricks topped, tarpaulins stripped and made up and the wooden hatch covers stacked on deck. The Gunlayer soon got the Fire Watch roster pinned up in our mess-room. I was on duty the first night with one of the soldiers. Some of the American dockers were talkative and wanted to know about the extent of the destruction of our cities. Most of them had sons and daughters stationed in England or training in Australia for the assault on the Japanese occupied Islands in the Pacific. It always seemed strange to be in port with no blackout restrictions – the ship lit up as well as the cranes and the wharf and warehouses. But the prettiest sight was the New York skyline and all the traffic.

I went ashore as I had done previously with Stan and Eddie, the Maritime gunners, and young Tommy from Birmingham.

Again we made straight for the Stage Door Canteen. A lady recognised us and when we told her we were engaged in supplying the American servicemen based in Australia she was pleased to talk with us as her son was out there. We then went to the Paramount Theatre in Times Square and saw a famous Country and Western Singer, Chill Wills. He was very tall, 6' 3", and looked smart in his Western outfit and huge white Stetson hat. He was a truly popular entertainer and received rapturous applause from all the audience. We returned to the Stage Door Canteen for some good American hospitality and then back to our Ship.

Working round the clock the dockers quickly loaded all holds. Thousands of tons of war supplies, including cases of food and refrigerated meat. When we sailed I did not realise that it would be the last time I would see America until after the war.

Once again we had an uneventful passage across the vast expanse of the

Pacific Ocean. Gun watches twenty-four hours a day but we had plenty of sunbathing. To sight another ship and to witness the exchange of Morse was something of a novelty. Just after we passed through Sydney Heads we were stowing ammunition away when I slipped on the wet deck whilst holding a 4" shell. I kept a good grip on it to prevent it sliding along the deck, but I landed heavily and in doing so suffered a nasty painful hernia in my right groin. The P.O. sent me along to see the Ship's doctor who informed me that I would have to go ashore and be operated on or else wear a truss. "What is a truss, sir" I asked, never having heard of hernias or trusses before. He then showed me one and I took one look at it and said I would rather have the operation! He told me to pack my kit and be prepared to sign off as soon as we had berthed.

The following day the Second Mate informed me that Naval Transport would collect me before mid-day. I said a sad farewell to all my mates, sailors, Master, etc. I signed off on June 24th. I had served as Gunlayer on "Orestes" for seven and a half months. She was a happy and well-run ship and the food was excellent thanks to the two Chinese cooks.

Transport arrived and the lads carried my gear down to the wharf. So a quick handshake and away to Rushcutters Bay, Royal Naval Australian Hospital. At Rushcutters Bay they quickly got me organised into a small sick bay for four in the hospital grounds and I was told that I would be admitted to the Main Hospital the following day.

The other occupant in the sick bay was a young wartime Australian sailor who had a stomach problem. He produced two mugs of tea and we got through a few cigarettes together. We had to collect our meals and eat on our own in this small room. The weather was quite warm but I soon discovered that the pain of a hernia is tiring so I had to lie down. An Australian paper was to hand and that made some good reading. The evening meal came round. I do remember this, as it was steak and chips, bread and real butter! A nurse came over from the Main Hospital and informed me to get my kit locked away after breakfast and report to a particular Ward at 9 a.m. I had a bad night and really missed my ship and shipmates.

The next day I reported to a huge Ward and was allocated a bed by a pretty young Australian Wren. About 10 o'clock I had a visit from a Naval Doctor who was to perform the operation, a Lieutenant Commander Flemming. After an examination he told me I would be given a light meal at 6 p.m. and he would operate the following day.

The Ward was very long and wide but there were plenty of Nurses, Wrens and male nurses. There was a friendly and pleasant atmosphere and we were allowed to smoke. My neighbour in the next bed was a regular Australian Petty Officer who had undergone a stomach operation but he was good storyteller. Some voluntary workers came round with free fruit drinks, sweets and reading material. All in all it was a happy Ward.

The following morning I was wheeled into a room next to the Operating Theatre. Lt.Commander Flemming informed me that I was not going to have a general anaesthetic but a spinal one. I received an injection half way up my spine and told to raise both my legs. When they fell down on to the trolley they took me into the Operating theatre. They placed a sort of gauze over my eyes but it rested on the tip of my nose enabling me to see everything that took place. There was the Lt. Commander and three Wren nurses. An incision was made and then the offending part was pushed back inside me followed by a surgical sewing job. I remember being wheeled back into the Ward when I then went to sleep.

Lt. Commander Flemming came to see me that evening and I thanked him for taking care of me. The not very encouraging news was that I had to remain flat on my back for three weeks. I was just given an extra pillow at meal times. This makes one feel really helpless – a daily bed bath and a massage to prevent bedsores, not forgetting bottle and bedpans! However, there was nice food and I received lots of attention from the Wren nurses.

The only sad subject that came up was the disappearance of the Cruiser H.M.A.S. Sydney. This was a complete mystery until I learned the true facts many years later from a retired Merchant Seaman friend now living in Australia. His Uncle, a Merchant Seaman and Tug Master of H.M.A.S. Hero, was ordered to go and make a search for her. He found the area where she had sunk but to his dismay and horror he did find floating around sailors caps, and the tubular Naval issue life-belts, the rubber blow-up type, and three Carley floats. These were riddled with machine gun bullets from the Japanese submarine that had been re-fuelling alongside the German "Q" ship "Kormaran" disguised as a Dutch freighter. The "Kormaran" cleverly got to a distance of 900 metres then opened up with her devastating fire power and underwater torpedo tubes. The "Kormaran" had to be abandoned when she caught fire, due to the brave crew of H.M.A.S. Sydney who inflicted a lot of damage and caused an oil fire which got out of control. The Kormaran's crew made the West Coast of Australia. The Japanese U-boat dived but surfaced again to machine-gun the crew of H.M.A.S. Sydney. She then went on her way to a rendezvous off Pearl Harbour to pick up Japanese pilots after the bombing of Pearl Harbour. At this date the Japanese were not in the war.

When I was in Hospital discussing H.M.A.S. Sydney I tried to take my neighbour's mind off the sad subject and told him of the time I had shot down a Japanese dive-bomber when they attacked the ships in Ceylon harbour on April 5th 1942. "Good on yer, Mate" he said. He must have told others in the Ward because I seemed to receive even more kind attention from the Wren nurses.

My stay in Hospital was longer than three weeks. After lying flat on my back all this time I then had to learn to walk again. This took a few days to master and I was accompanied by a nurse, otherwise I would have fallen over. The day of discharge came round and I thanked all the staff for making me fit again. I was taken to a fairly big Recuperative Centre where the doctor in charge informed me that my hernia was classified as a "heavy industrial" one and could take up to three months to heal properly. The good news was that my legs and knees required plenty of sun so at every opportunity that came my way I stretched out on the beach and soaked up the sun.

One of the Wren nurses was allowed to accompany me to the beach. She was very pretty and lots of fun and once a week she would take me to a small Greek restaurant and we would both have a large T-bone steak, chips and two eggs. She would never let me pay but I remember at that time the

meal cost five shillings (and this included bread and butter, tea and ice cream!).
There were servicemen of all nationalities in the Centre, quite a lot from the
Pacific Theatre of war and some of them had the most horrific injuries.

The time to leave came around and I said a grateful thank you to everyone,
and a sad goodbye to the Wren nurse who had become a true friend. Some
of my mates helped me to load my hammock and kit bags on to the Navy
transport that took me down to the docks. I then got a Navy launch out
into the harbour to join a Fort Boat that was swinging round her port an-
chor.

Names of Master, Officers, Crew and Gunners of M.V. "Orestes"

P. Purkis	Master
R.T. Harris	Mate
R.T. Crake	Second Mate
J.D. Evans	Third Mate
T. Johnstone	Extra. Third Mate
H. Cowley	Cadet
J.M. Pearce	"
F. Geoffrey	"
A.J. Brechowen	"
R. Carlton	"
T.R. Jones	Chief Engineer
L. Sullivan	Second Engineer
J. Buchan	Extra Second Engineer
W. Marshall	Third Engineer
R.K. Stephens	Fourth Engineer
R. Clark	Assistant Engineer
H. Bone	" "
A.O. Cook	" "
A. Wishart	" "
R. Wilkinson	First Electrician
A.J. Beard	Second Electrician
R.A. Mooney	First Radio Officer

R.D. Robinson	Second Radio Officer
G. Herringshaw	Third Radio Officer
E.L. Williams	Ship's Surgeon
S. Galway	Chief Steward
J.H. Adams	Second Steward
F. Henderson	Carpenter
H. Wainwright	Bosun
R.G. Griffith	Leading Seaman
E. Bradshaw	A/B
L. Bailey	A/B
M. Simpson	A/B
C. Camp	A/B
B. Evans	A/B
J. Corcoran	A/B
L. Broughton	A/B
C. Doyle	A/B
W. Morris	A/B
F. Hanna	A/B
J. Barlow	Senior Ordinary Seaman
A.G. Kellock	Junior Ordinary Seaman
H. Maddox	Deck Boy
A.D. Lamb	Deck Boy
R. Weston	Deck Boy

D.E.M.S. Gunners

C. Parrott	P/O Gunlayer
G. Grassick	A/B Gunlayer
J. Radford	Seaman Gunner
T. Sutton	Seaman Gunner
C. Bennett	Seaman Gunner
T. Waldron	Seaman Gunner

W. Watchorn   Seaman Gunner

Maritime Ack Ack Gunners

J. Wilson   L/Corporal
S. Sylvester   Gunner
A. Hawkins   Gunner
J. Hoyle   Gunner
H. Smith   Gunner

Note: There were two Chinese cooks whose names are not listed. Chinese crew members always signed on at the Company's Head Office in Liver Buildings, Liverpool.

M.V. Fort McDonnell

Chapter 13

M.V. FORT MCDONNELL

Built at Burrand Dry Dock, Esquimalt, North Vancouver, 1944.
Gross Tons: 6,693. Ministry of War Transport.
The M.V. Fort McDonnell survived the war.
In 1947 she was renamed "Cliffside"
In 1951 she was renamed "Cavodoro"
In 1953 she was renamed "Captain Luicis"
The Marine News of 1955, page 165, mentioned her last name above. There is no date of her going to the breakers yard.

It was the 7th October 1944 when I signed on M.V. "Fort McDonnell". I had been ashore for a total of 3 months 14 days, in hospital and convalescence. However, I had the satisfaction of once again being fit and able, and could play soccer, swim and box.

The Army and Navy Gunners gave me a hand to get aboard and along to our accommodation which was in the tween decks aft.

After getting acquainted with my new shipmates over a mug of tea, the Gunlayer in Charge, a wartime Petty Officer named George Snell, took me along to the saloon and I signed on. The Master's name was Grey and I found out later that he was known as "Slogger Grey", reputed as being handy with his fists! He was a man of few words and it was the usual "Welcome aboard".

The complement of D.E.M.S. Gunners was six. P.O. Gunlayer George Snell, myself Gunlayer, and four seaman Gunners. The Army Gunners numbered four, which included a Corporal from London. Because we were a new ship we had been fitted out with some modern equipment. A brand new 4" dual-purpose gun, which used fixed ammunition for submarines or aircraft. It also had a protective special shield around it. This was good for protection against shrapnel and quite a change from the obsolete old World War I guns we had been using. The stern had been strengthened to accommodate the 4" gun.

The Bofor was mounted on a raised platform abaft the 4". On the forecastle head the 12-pounder ack-ack gun had been mounted. We also had the 20 mm Oerlikon ack-ack guns mounted on the Bridge and boat deck, and a couple of 303 machine guns and smoke floats.

Part of our equipment was two very large barges, one on each side that were used to ferry supplies to H.M. ships of the Pacific Fleet. We carried two Merchant Seamen whose duty it was to act as coxswains of the barges to ferry the NAAFI stores around. The Indian crew did the loading under the supervision of the Indian Boson, or Sarang. The seamen, greaser and wipers were all Indian, as were the Stewards, Cooks and Galley Boy. The Indian crew had their own galley right aft below the 4" gun deck.

The day after I signed on the Master ordered boat and fire drill, followed by gun drill. The Second Mate, Mr. Mathews, was the Gunnery Officer. We upped anchor and sailed late afternoon on 8th October 1944.

Our passage was all the way across the "Great Australian Bight" and, as we expected, it was a very rough sea. We dropped anchor off Free Mantle. The crew and coxswains were kept busy supplying all manner of H.M. ships, cruisers, destroyers, corvettes and submarines. Every hold in the ship had been partitioned off with a stairway right down to the lower holds. We were a gigantic NAAFI store ship. Food, clothes, cigarettes, tobacco and even large demi-Johns of neat Navy rum, holding 3-10 gallons and encased in wicker baskets with carrying handles. In charge of the NAAFI stores was a Royal Navy Reserve Officer, Lt. Prichard, and to assist him was a wartime Leading Seaman Writer and two Seaman Writers. He also had a civilian NAAFI Assistant, "Big Jim", a Yorkshireman. After continuously supplying many and various ships, we received our sailing orders for Bombay. We quickly discovered that a gigantic invasion fleet was being assembled round the Indian coast, another great armada of ships, troops and barges for the invasion of Singapore. "Operation Zipper" was the code word to knock hell out of the Japanese. Once again I said farewell to everyone and I signed off on 19th July 1945 in Bombay.

Names of Master, Officers, Crew and Gunners of M.V. "Fort McDonnell"

F. Grey	Master
N.P. Smith	Chief Mate
M. Matthews	Second Mate
J. Owen	Third Mate
I.G. Clements	Cadet
D.B. Swanson	Cadet
N. Elford	Cadet
G.C. Jones	Cadet
G. Crawford	Chief Engineer
D.G. Stuart	Second Engineer
N.V. Fenny	Asst. Second Engineer
R.S. Parker	Third Engineer
H.M. Faithy	Fourth Engineer
I.A. Sullivan	Assistant Engineer
L.F. Flower	Assistant Engineer
V. Hollingworth	Electrician
S.L. Bhat	Doctor
R. Borrell	First Radio Officer
C. Woodcock	Second Radio Officer
J. Bramhall	Third Radio Officer
E.C. Price	Carpenter

The Boson, Sailors, Engine Room Greasers and Wipers, Cooks and Stewards - all Calcutta Indians.

G. Swindells	Quarter Master
H. Forsythe	Quarter Master
L. Cummings	Quarter Master
E. Kelly	Quarter Master
P. Ransom	Quarter Master

(The Quarter Masters also manned the two NAAFI supply barges to ferry supplies to ships of the Pacific Fleet)

W. Cordsley	Chief Steward
S. Grieve	Second Steward
A. Pritchard	Chief Clerk NAAFI staff
G. Morgan	Supply Stores NAAFI
R. Nickson	Supply Stores NAAFI
T. Smithers	Supply Stores NAAFI
T.C. Tuiberfuede	Supply Stores NAAFI

D.E.M.S. Gunners

G. Snell	P.O. Gunlayer
G. Grassick	A/B Gunlayer
T. Halloran	A/B Seaman Gunner
W. Carr	A/B Seaman Gunner
W. Lee	A/B Seaman Gunner
H. McFarland	A/B Seaman Gunner

Maritime Ack-Ack Gunners

A. Duece	L/Corporal
E. Walker	
A.Roberts	
E. Emslie	

M. V. Cilicia

Chapter 14

M.V. CILICIA

Built for the Anchor Line Glasgow by Fairfields of Govan in 1938.
Gross tonnage: 11,157
Port of Registry: Glasgow
Official Number: 165934

In October 1939 she was commissioned as an A.M.C. (Armed Merchant Cruiser)
In 1944 she became a Troopship.
May 1947 she re-entered her passenger service for Anchor Donaldson Line. After the war the Cilicia had a complete refit and re-entered the Indian passenger service.In November 1965 she was sold to a Dutch concern and used as a floating hostel for training stevedores and was renamed the Jan Backx. In August 1980 she was towed to Bilbao to be broken up.

There was a lot of activity at the R.N. Barracks in Bombay. I knew my way around, as I had been here before when I signed off M.V. Pardo in September 1942. The accommodation was very roomy with 24 to a billet. There were electric fans and we all had mosquito nets over our bunks.
On my first night I managed to get into the City to see a film. Later I was put on a refresher course which took five days and included all the latest armaments, the modern 4" dual-purpose gun with protective shield, and the Oerlikon 20 mm. I had another run through on the 6" surface gun. I did not have any guard duties as I had reported to sick bay with a sprained ankle.
On 1st August 1945 I was posted to the Troopship M.V. "Cilicia". Captain Edward Stormont was the Master..
There were a lot of D.E.M.S. and Maritime Gunners aboard.. The accommodation was reasonable, one section for the Navy and one for the Army, with separate messrooms so we had Petty Officers and Army Sargeants. The

Officer in Charge of all the gunners was Lt. Commander Cleghorn, R.N.Z. Navy and R.N. Reserve. He was a giant of a man and a body building fanatic. He did his workout on the boat deck and always had a lot of WREN observers (to bed with a wren and up with a lark). He insisted that all of us gunners took part every day before breakfast and no one was excused. Now fully recovered from my operation, I was glad of the exercise to get my body back to its former fitness. The food aboard was of a higher standard than some of the ships I had served on and appreciated by us all.

I was assigned to one of the 6" gun crews. It was a change from the small 4" guns I had grown used to.

We were fully loaded with soldiers and our destination was to be Singapore. Yes, the invasion of Singapore, code name "Operation Zipper", and the date was to be announced. All gunners were issued with a rifle so that we could go ashore and fight should the Japanese sink the ship. What we did not know at the time was that Sir Winston Churchill and President Harry Truman were working on a date to test the new super weapon on Japan, the atomic bomb, known at the time as "Fat Boys" because of their cylindrical appearance.

We had finished breakfast one morning when the Master's voice boomed over the intercom "Attention All Hands, this is the Master speaking". He went on to say "The war is over, I say again, the war is over". "The Americans have attacked two Japanese cities with a new type of bomb and the Emperor has decided to negotiate for peace". "All fighting to cease before Tokyo gets devastated and reduced to rubble". You could have heard a pin drop and then there was a deafening roar of approval, followed by talk of at last getting back to the U.K.

The powers that be in the Far Eastern Command quickly got things organised before the end of the day. All troops quickly disembarked, then along came a large group of Medical Officers, both Army and Navy, men and women, and a lot of orderlies. A load of tinned food was also taken aboard.

We upped anchor and sailed. The Master once again announced over the tanoy that we were proceeding down the Straits of Malaya to Port Dixon to bring back our soldiers who had been marched and herded into prisoner of war camps. You will see by the photographs how they were made to suffer under the Japanese army. We kept our rifles and were posted all the way round the ship to explode any mines as a channel was being swept by four minesweepers ahead of us. We also had two Destroyers. After making fast, it did not take long for our soldiers who were prisoners of war to arrive at the wharf. Some walking and some on stretchers. I say this with the deepest respect for them "the walking and the living dead". It was a sight one can never forget. There were a lot of tears and misty eyes on seeing these men. On our way back to India, Vizagabatan, the stories we heard about conditions in the camps and the way our soldiers were treated was unbelievable. I am sorry I just cannot print it all, flogging, beating, beheading were just a few of the things they had to endure.

After disembarking the soldiers we went back to Port Dixon for a second load. These we took to Madras.

It was here in Madras that I signed off on 30th August 1945. I then travelled by train to Calcutta and from there all the way to Bombay.

M.V. Staffordshire

Chapter 15

M.V. STAFFORDSHIRE

Built by Fairfields Ship Builders, Glasgow in 1928 for the Bibby-Line, Liver-
pool.
Gross tons: 10,654
Official Number: 161082
Port of Registry: Liverpool
In April 1940 she became a Troopship.
In March 1941 the M V Staffordshire was bombed, abandoned and beached.
She was eventually re-floated, towed round to the Tyne and repaired.
She then returned as a Troopship.
After signing off M.V. "Cilicia" at Madras, I travelled by rail to Calcutta
and all the way to Bombay. What a rough journey these troop trains were.
Open sided. Overpowering heat during the day, and freezing cold at night.
Fortunately, stopovers were well organised by the O.C. Transport and our
meals consisted of thick bully beef and cheese sandwiches, and plenty of
tea. There were also free cigarettes, and anyone with spare rupees could
buy a large coconut slice, which were very popular.
I signed on M.V. "Staffordshire" on 6th September 1945, the Master being
Captain H. Brady. This was my tenth wartime ship. I was really upset
when I discovered that she was not going to England, as the Gunnery
Officer on the "Cilicia", Lt. Commander Cleghorn, had told me that my demob
number implied that I was to be posted to a Troopship bound for the U.K.
I went along to see the Gunnery Officer who was very young and new out from
England. He told me to state my case which I quickly did, saying that I had left
England on 9th October 1943 and that by the time I arrived back in the U.K. I
would have been away for two years. He assured me that he would go ashore
to D.E.M.S. H.Q. and get the mix up sorted out.
My only consolation was that with the war now over there were no gun watches.
Everyone was on day work. This meant turning to at 09.00 hours after break-

fast, getting all the ammunition re-packed into their boxes ready to be offloaded. I thought it would have been quicker to dump it all overboard, but the powers that be wanted it all put into mothballs, no doubt thinking that some Dictator somewhere in the world would flex his muscles and start a war and the killing all over again.

After getting the ammunition boxed and labelled, our next job was moving or carrying Servicemen to various ports to be put aboard Troopships returning to the U.K. Where they all came from I do not know but there was just one never ending stream of soldiers, sailors and airmen of all different nationalities who were destined for the invasion of Japan. I discovered in later years that in human lives this would have cost over two million young men and women. I do not know how this figure was arrived at if it was true, but I thank Harry Truman for dropping the two "Fat Boys" on Hiroshima and Nagasaki.

After five years and 11 months of fighting and seeing your mates killed, and hearing the cries of drowning seamen who could not be helped because of atrocious sea conditions, it was now time to get to grips with ones self and decide what you would do after de-mobilisation. Most of us wondered if we would have a job to go back to and what the wage structure would be. I had already decided that I would not be going back to farm work. I would return home to visit my Aunt and Uncle and have a reunion with the family but I would then steer a quick course for Liverpool and re-join the Merchant Navy.

We didn't know how the new Government under Clement Attlee would tackle the mammoth task of rebuilding our bombed cities and docks. The majority of servicemen overseas were sorry at losing our great wartime leader Winston Churchill, particularly so as thousands out in the Far East did not get a chance to vote.

I signed off in Calcutta on 8th October 1945.

The "Empress of Scotland"
Built by Fairfields of Govan for the Canadian Pacific Steamship Company in 1929

Chapter 16

EMPRESS OF SCOTLAND

Built by Fairfields of Govan for the Canadian Pacific Steamship Company in 1929.

Gross tons: 26,032

Official No: 161082

She was originally named the "Empress of Japan".

She broke the record for crossing the Pacific and in November 1939 she was requisitioned and converted into a troopship.

In November 1940 she was attacked by enemy aircraft in the North Sea but was not hit.

Up to the time Japan entered the war, ships were not allowed to be re-named. Winston Churchill said this was nonsense and someone came up with "Empress of Scotland".

It was on 16th October 1942 when she was renamed.

In 1948 she was returned to her owners after steaming 600,000 miles on war service, and was refitted by the builders for the North Atlantic Service. 1950 was her first post-war sailing.

In November 1957 she was laid up and in 1958 she was sold to Hamburg Atlantic Line and re-named the "Hanseatic". She was rebuilt but one of her funnels was disposed of for more deck space. Her tonnage was also increased to 30,030 gross tons.

In September 1966 she caught fire in New York and was towed to Hamburg. There the surveyors said she was beyond repair and in December 1966 she was broken up.

After signing off M.V. Staffordshire on 8th October 1945 in Calcutta, and into barracks, the heat was unbelievable. The coolest place was the NAAFI Canteen and, hopefully, to enjoy some ice-cold Tennants beer. The main topic of conversation was, of course, demob. I heard that most of us would be going overland to Bombay and wait in barracks there for a UK bound ship.

The following day, having no guard duties, I took a rickshaw into Calcutta.

There was much poverty and beggars everywhere. Market stalls selling cheap jewellery and trinkets; a snake charmer, "watch the mongoose kill the cobra"; fortune-tellers, and much more. The pavements were filthy because of the habit of spitting beetle juice everywhere. I quickly decided to get back to barracks.

I scanned the 'movements board' and there it was – tomorrow 10th October I was to join an early troop train for Bombay. Transport arrived at 08.00 to take me to the station. I had very little packing to do but I made sure I had plenty of cigarettes and I also bought some chocolate for an emergency.

I do not remember how many carriages were attached to the train but it was a mighty coal- burning monster, probably built in England. At the front there were four covered carriages, all the remaining ones were open-sided but with safety bars fitted to prevent one from falling onto the tracks. There was a central corridor. The seating arrangements were for three on each side of the gangway and facing, making a total of twelve, so there was plenty of conversation going on. The carriages very quickly got hot, but no one seemed to care, plenty of reminiscing about the war and talk of what one would do after demob. The stopovers were very well organised as I had come to expect. Thick sandwiches with either cheese or bully beef, along with tea. Again, there were Indian traders selling bags of peanuts and thick coconut slices that were good value.

This was a vast Continent we had to cross. Calcutta is situated in the Indian Ocean at the top of the Bay of Bengal where many merchant ships have met their fate. The train took a southwesterly track across to Bombay situated on the West Coast and the Arabian Sea. A distance of about 1200 miles. What magnificent scenery we passed through. It was a beautiful sight to see the tea plantations and the workers gathering the tea crop. We saw large white painted country style estate houses, homes of the owners.

We finally arrived in Bombay at the end of that marathon overland journey on 13th October. We were transported by army lorries to a huge camp some miles outside of Bombay, which was where we had to wait for a UK bound troopship. The billets were big and accommodated 24. A good bed with mosquito nets and plenty of fans. The food was also good and a lot of

'McOnackies' stew was served. Now the war was over there must have been thousands, or probably millions, of tins around. Not forgetting the dehydrated cabbage and potato powder - it tasted fairly good mashed with butter. We also got used to the American dried egg powder that was a good substitute when eggs were scarce. There was a NAAFI Canteen which sold Tennants beer but money was short and I had to manage on £2 and five shillings a week.

The day after I entered this huge camp, there was an outbreak of bubonic plague in a local village, so everyone had to have a quick inoculation and we were not allowed out of the main gate. We saw from the enclaves of our camp, soldiers going into the village and burning it to the ground with flame-throwers. We never found out the extent of the plague.

To while away our time we played soccer and went on country rambles. There was also an organised trip to a local dairy farm where the cows were all Dutch Friesians. I was not impressed with the cleanliness of the cows and milking parlour compared to our farm back home, but the overseer did not think this was important.

After 11 days of camp life my posting came through. I was to join the "Empress of Scotland", Bombay Harbour. On the 24th October 1945 I went aboard this large passenger ship and I was allocated a bunk on the second deck down. The food on board was only just passable. It seemed to be a never-ending series of 'queasy' meals. To help pass the time films were shown, but this wasn't a success because the screen could not be kept still due to high winds!

The Master's name was J.W. Thomas and he addressed us over the intercom. He said that if the weather was favourable he would have us back home in less than three weeks.

The weather did hold good and we arrived and made fast at the Pier Liverpool on 9th November 1945, a crossing of 16 days. We all felt a big disappointment that there was no "welcome home" to greet us. I had served the last two years of the war in the Pacific and Far East, and along with my earlier service this made a total of three years and three months service away from the UK. However, it felt great to be back in Liverpool and the Transport took me and a few of the other gunners up to our D.E.M.S. barracks at the top of Brownlow Hill.

I was told that the following day I would be going on leave.

I got smartened up and took a stroll down to Lime Street. This was all so different from when I was last home – no blackout restrictions or air raids to worry about - it was good to be there. I took in a film and treated myself to a fish and chip supper.

The following morning I took a taxi and got my two kit bags and hammock down to Lime Street station and put them in the 'Left Luggage'. I reported to Liver Building and met a very friendly WREN Writer who worked out my leave and back pay, which was a fair amount. I then caught the train to Chesterfield and arrived home on the afternoon of 10th November.

Both my brother and sister had survived the war, also one of my Uncle's, a Transport Driver RAF, and two cousins who were with the Eighth Army. Two of my schoolmates had been killed at sea while serving with the Royal Navy and two who were in the Army; another was killed while serving with the Royal Air Force.

It was over two years since I had last been home and I felt really happy to be with the family again. A few parties and "get together" plans were organised for Christmas. All I had to do now was wait and count the days until I could sling my uniform in for civvies. This turned out to be a pre-war Montague Burton 3-piece suit to the value of £4 and 10 shillings!

Homeward bound British Ex. Prisoners of War pass up the gangway of a troopship.

Royal Marine Band from H.M.S.. Sussex came ashore at Singapore to entertain British POW's and Civilian internees awaiting ships for home. The band was given a great reception and the Audience heard all the latest dance tunes.

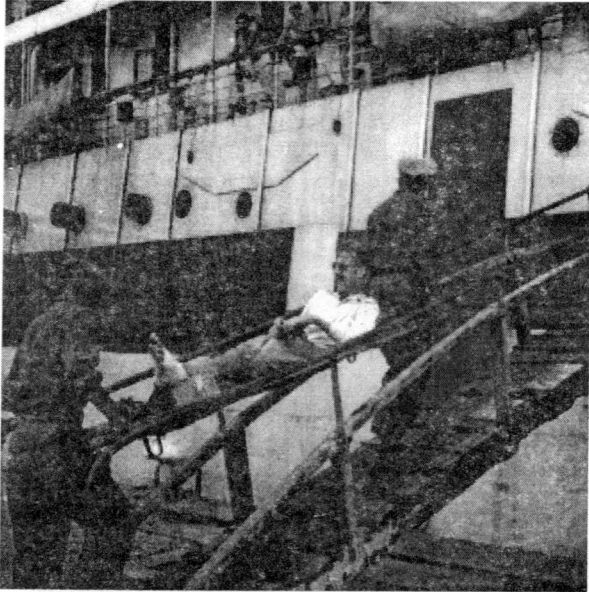

Bound for home. A wounded released POW is carried aboard a hospital ship at Singapore

The dockside scene viewed from the hospital ship. Stretcher cases arrive by Ambulance.

Wounded and sick released POW's go home by stretcher. Boarding a hospital ship at Singapore.

Released POW's and civilian internees board a hospital ship at Singapore

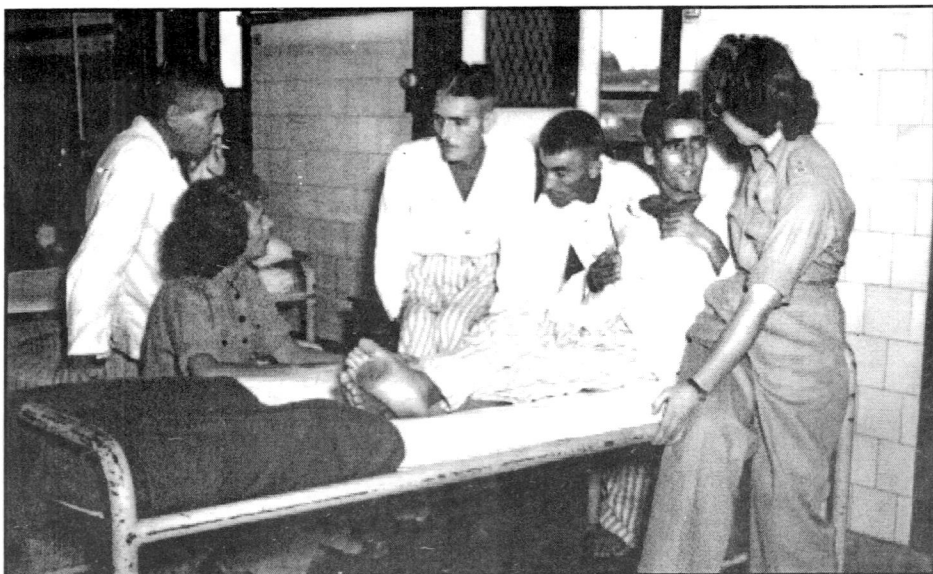

Two nurses talk with Ex/POW's removed to a Singpore hospital.

A convoy of released POW's leaving Chagi Jail En-Route for the hospital ship.

At Singapore released POW's and civilian internees invited aboard the Cruiser H.M.S. Sussex.

Japanese POW's made to push their transport up Changi Road.

Close up of a Japanese POW. he wears gloves.

Left to right. Mr. W.V.Simpson of Union Grove, Aberdeen, Mr. H. Collins of 11 Lapsley Place, Liverpool. Mr. J. Lindfield of 13 Martell Road, W/Dulwich, London, Three merchant Navy men, chatting to the Matron and Sister (Quarnnev) of the Hospital ship "Amarapoore" in Singapore harbour waiting to take sick prisoners home.

Above
Left to right ACIS
Roberts of Mancot
Lane, Queen ferry,
Chester, LAC Hadow
of 5 North Parade,
Grantham, Lincs.,
LAC L.D. Gilham PF
63, Malvern Road,
Leytonstone, E. 11
A.C.A. Armstrong of
218 Kingsway.

D.E.M.S. Gunners manning the Six inch gun. My very last ship. The "M.V. CILICIA", I was in the six inch gun crew. Standing by for the invasion of Singapore "Operation Zipper" Harry S. Truman dropped the Two "Fat Boys" on the Nippons. So we quickly disembarked all the troops and we were the first ship down the straits to get our soldiers out and back to India. I did so much want to fire that monster of a gun.

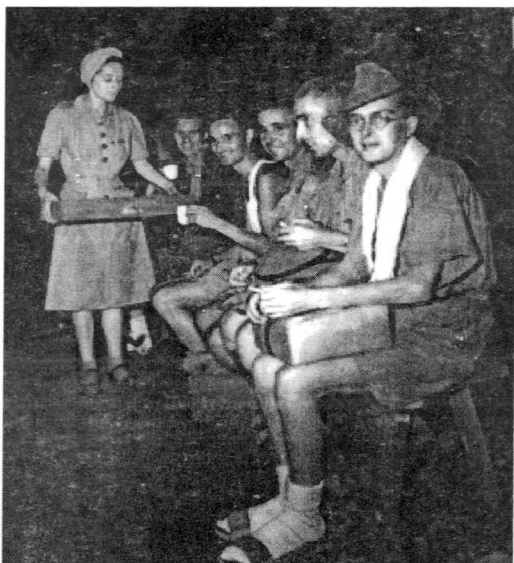

Released from Jail POW's are greeted by nurses at the dockside and given tea.

A close up of Corporal Johnson of 7 Sandhurst Road, Kingsbury N.W.9 Taken before he boarded a home-ward troopship at Singapore.

(3)   Similar figures, from Trade Division records, for fishing vessels, estuary craft lost by enemy action for the whole period of the war are :

Number of vessels lost		Total crew (including D.E.M.S.) in vessels lost		No. of crew lost (including D.E.M.S.) in vessels lost		Pro crε veε
U-Boat	By all enemy causes	By U-Boat	By all enemy causes	By U-Boat	By all enemy causes	By U-Boa
25	189	294	1,606	90	784	% 31

The higher proportion of crews lost in small craft by all enemy cause for by the fact that a large number of the small craft (particularly fishing vess by mines or aircraft, and the chances of survival of the crews were in such circ than in the larger vessels.

Rescue Ships

(1)   Ships fitted specially for rescue and accommodation of survivors were br with convoys in January, 1941. These vessels, being of a small and handy ty to arrive quickly at the scene of a casualty in a convoy and so perform invalu: picking up survivors and attending to the medical cases as the following figui

(2)   Up to June, 1945, some 4,183 survivors were picked up by 29 rescue sh survivors 2,302 were British, 951 United States citizens, 369 Norwegians, 14 Russians, 72 Dutch and 246 other Nationals including 4 Germans from a U-B

(3)   Rescue ships performed 796 voyages in attendance on convoys, covering : 2,250,000 miles.

(4)   Six ships were lost on actual rescue service.

Foreign Trade—Shipping Movement at U.K. Ports
Average Monthly Entrances and Clearances in the years 1935-1944

(Thousand Net Tons)

Year	Entered in the Foreign Trade		Cleared in the Foreign '	
	With Cargo	In Ballast	With Cargo	I
1935	5,302	1,826	4,777	
1936	5,618	1,779	4,735	

3)   Light machine guns (.303 in. and .30 in.) were the first weapons to be pro quantity during 1940 and 1941. It was not until mid-1942, however, that Oerli became plentiful ; some 12,000 had been mounted by June, 1943, and from t this number increased rapidly to 22,000 by the end of 1944.

9)   In addition to guns, various deterrents such as the P.A.C.(D) and kite and used, and continued in use in coastal waters and in ships taking part in operat the Normandy landings.

0)   *Personnel.*—The manning problem was also difficult and, in the critical d fall of France, various measures were taken to raise trained men. From the ori of 1,300 R.N. and R.M. Pensioners, no fewer than five different organised bodies into existence during 1940. These were D.E.M.S. ratings (R.N. and R.M.), the Guard, Army Machine-gun Teams, Army Port Gunners, and Merchant Navy Gu first four groups were in time merged into two—Naval D.E.M.S. ratings and Royal Artillery. By January, 1944, they totalled some 600 officers and 38,000 n 24,000 were Naval D.E.M.S. and 14,000 M.R.A. The sailors and soldiers were int and the complements of ships ranged from 60 in a large liner, 7 to 12 in a cargo : one man in a tug or small craft.

1)   The casualties incurred by D.E.M.S. and Maritime R.A. personnel from 3rd Sep to 8th May, 1945, were :—

	Naval	Maritime R. A.
Killed	2,531	1,151
Missing	182	71
Prisoners of War	168	74
	2,881	1,296

2)   *Training.*—The training of this large body of men was no mean problem ; out mostly ashore and was continuous. In addition to the D.E.M.S. service pe 150,000 merchant seamen were trained in handling guns and A.A. devices. As gressed firing practice at sea by merchant ships became a recognised custom.

3)   *Value of Defensive Equipment of Merchant Ships.*—The number of enemy down or damaged up to the end of hostilities was :—

	Confirmed	Probable	Damaged
By Merchant Ships and Fishing Vessels ...	158	51	120
Shared between Escorts and Merchant Ships ...	164	28	23

Statistics covering the period September 1942 to January 1945 also show that unescorted merchant ships attacked by U-Boat escaped.

But no figures can show the heartening effect or confidence inspired by defensive crews, nor the deterrent effect on the enemy's tactics and morale.

(See Diagram 1)

Net Defence

1)   Successful trials of this form of defence against torpedo attack fitted to a

SECRET

Number 1
12-1-42

W/T CALL SIGNS
Commodore (individual)   XU D 1.
Vice Commodore   "   XU D 2.
Whole Convoy   XU D.3.
Commodore's portion Convoy XU D 4.
Vice Commodore   "   "   XU D 5.
Senior Officer of Escort.XU D 6.
Rear Commodore portion Convoy XU D 7.

...ables.
...mns 3 cables

...ES.
...LING CASTLE.
..."CERES", "NORMAN"

Position
Speed &
Minimum

02	03	04	05.
21 B X M ...ONTES .154'	31 G R P Z STRATHNAVER 153'	41 G Y P X STIRLING CASTLE 157'	51 G S R Z STAFFORDSHIRE 142'
22 F K V ...RANTO 155' L.R.	32 G Y K S STRATHMORE 152'	42 B C J F EMPIRE WOODLARK 138' L.R.	52 G M N Z PARDO 90'
23 L V X ...EROY OF INDIA 156'	33 G D X F BRITANNIC 165' S.R.	43 P D K D CHRISTIAAN HUYGENS 160'	53 P C A H AAGTEKERK 134' S.R.
24	34	44	54

216

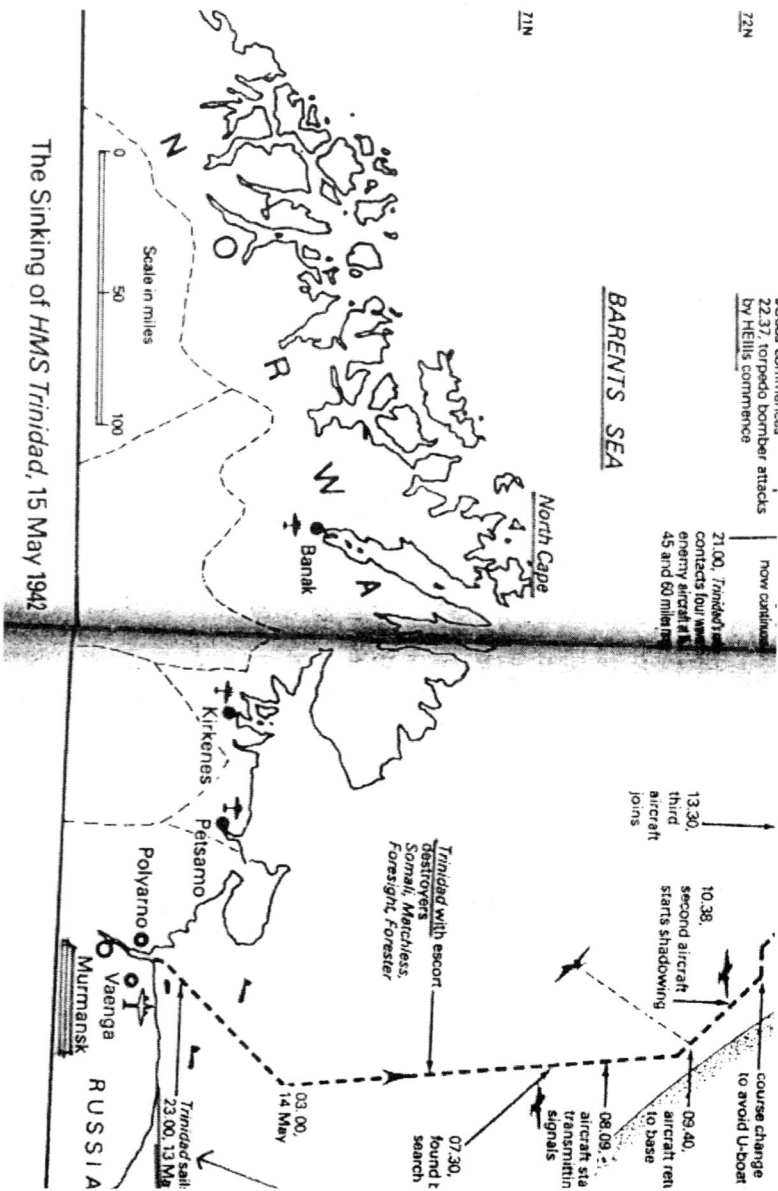

The Sinking of *HMS Trinidad*, 15 May 1942

BARENTS SEA

NORWAY

North Cape

Banak

Kirkenes

Petsamo

Polyarno

Vaenga

Murmansk

RUSSIA

Scale in miles

0   50   100

72N

71N

22.37, torpedo bomber attacks
by HEllis commence

now continues

21.00, *Trinidad*
contacts four
enemy aircraft at
45 and 60 miles

13.30,
third
aircraft
joins

10.38,
second aircraft
starts shadowing

09.40,
aircraft ret
to base

course change
to avoid U-boat

08.09, :
aircraft sta
transmittin
signals

07.30,
found t
search

Trinidad with escort
destroyers
*Somali, Matchless,
Foresight, Forester*

03.00,
14 May

Trinidad sail
23.00, 13 Ma

217

Actual convoy course with indication of convoy and Escort Group.

Convoy with close air support.

Course instructions with reference points and altered course instructions.

Stragglers' route.

Points/Routes deciphered by the 'B' Service.

U-boat position.

U-boat proceeding.

U-boat tanker.

Contact signals of U-boat.

Contact signals of German aircraft.

U-boat signal picked up by D/F.

U-boat reported by Allied aircraft.

Allied air reconnaissance.

Allied U-boat situation.

Patrol line.

Proposed line.

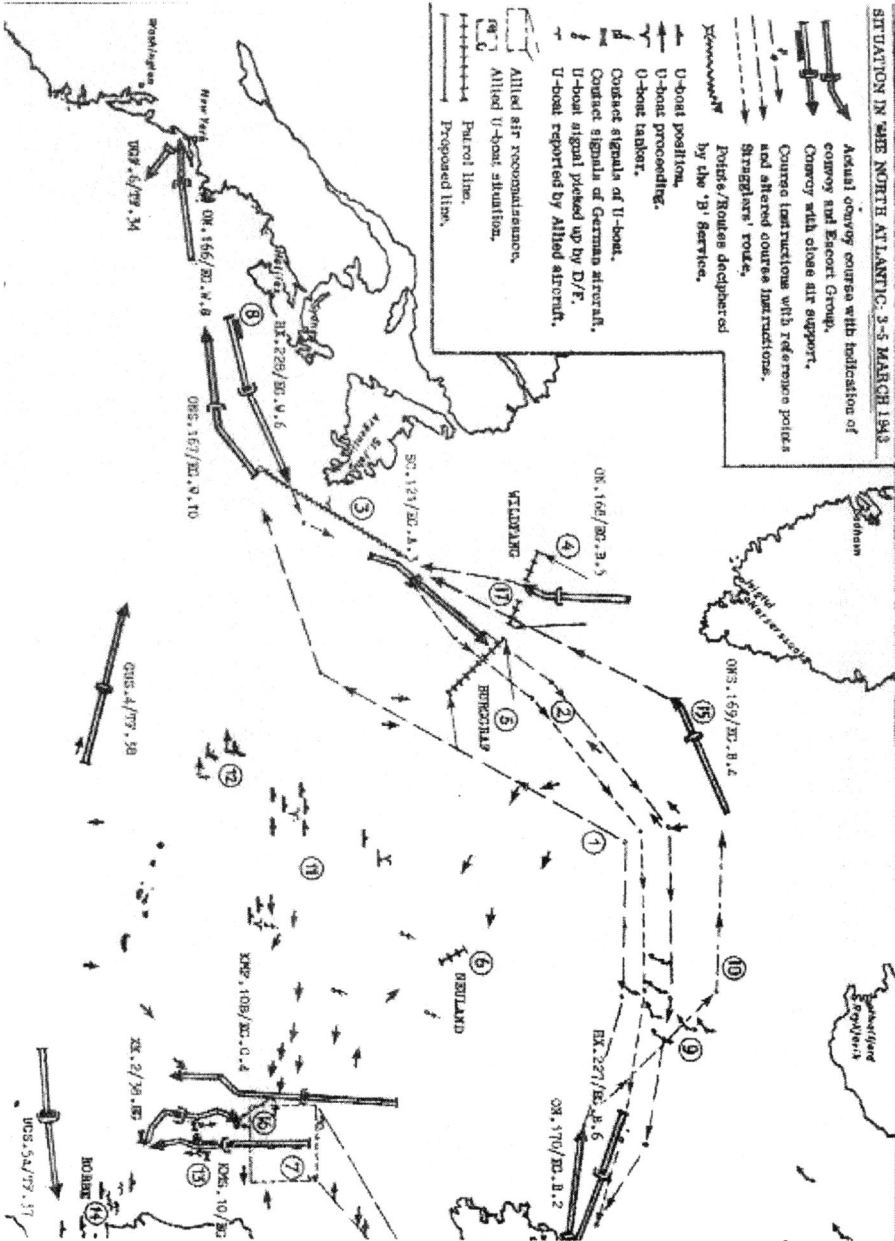

Washington

New York

UGF.6/TF.34

ON.166/ME.V.8

BX.228/ME.V.6

ONS.167/ME.V.10

SC.121/ME.A.3

ON.168/ME.B.5

WILDFANG

BURGGRAF

ONS.169/ME.B.4

CU5.4/TF.58

ON.170/ME.B.2

BX.227/ME.B.6

KMS.10B/ME.G.4

XK.2/39.HG

SEELÖWE

NELAND

UCS.5A/TF.57

HALIFAX

KMS.10/ME

218

TURN IN THE NORTH ATLANTIC, ...

Actual convoy course with indication of convoy and Escort Group.

Convoy with close air support.

Course instructions with reference points and altered course instructions.

Stragglers' route.

Points/Routes deciphered by the 'B' Service.

U-boat position.

U-boat proceeding.

U-boat tanker.

Contact signals of U-boat.

Contact signals of German aircraft.

U-boat signal picked up by D/F.

U-boat reported by Allied aircraft.

Allied air reconnaissance.

Allied U-boat situation.

Patrol line.

Proposed line.

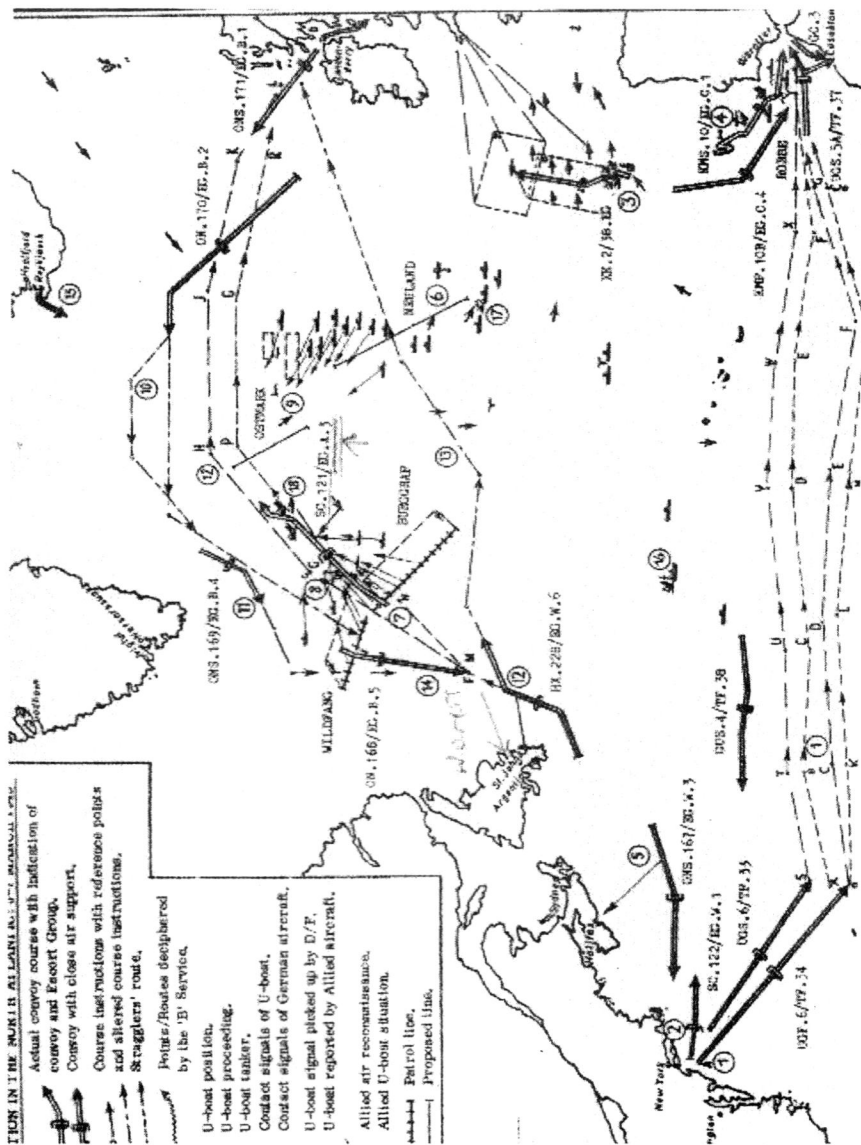

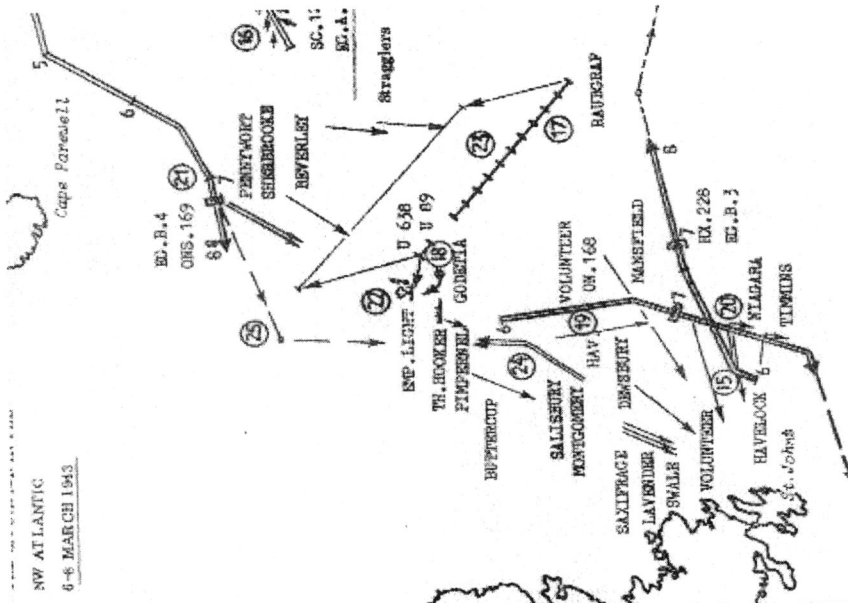

NW ATLANTIC
6-8 MARCH 1943

Cape Farewell

E.G.B.4
ONS.169

PENNYWORT
SHERBROOKE
BEVERLEY

Stragglers

SC.1?
E.G.A.

RAMSGRAY

U 638
U 89

EMP.LIGHT
TH.HOOKER
PIMPERNEL
GODETIA

VOLUNTEER
ON.168
MANSFIELD

HX.228
E.G.B.3

BUTTERCUP

SALISBURY
MONTGOMERY

HAV
DEMBETRY

NIAGARA
TIMMINS

SAXIFRAGE
LAVENDER
SWALE

VOLUNTEER

HAVELOCK
St. Johns

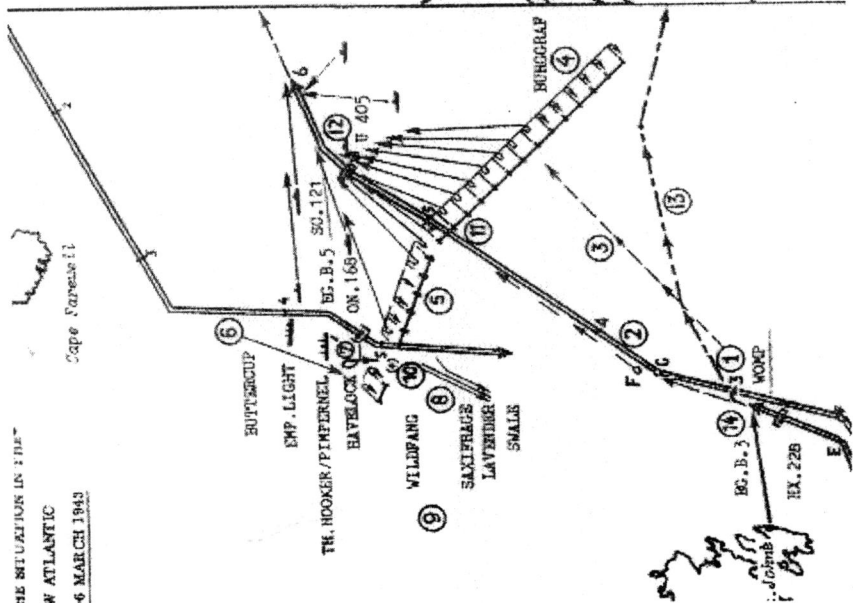

THE SITUATION IN THE
W ATLANTIC
4-6 MARCH 1943

Cape Farewell

U 405

MOROCRAP

SC.121
E.G.B.5
ON.168

BUTTERCUP
EMP.LIGHT
TH.HOOKER/PIMPERNEL
HAVELOCK

WILDFANG

SAXIFRAGE
LAVENDER
SWALE

WOMP

E.G.B.3
HX.228

St. Johns

SITUATION IN THE NORTH ATLANTIC: 7-9 MARCH 1943

Actual convoy course with indication of convoy and Escort Group.
Convoy with close air support.
Course instructions with reference points and altered course instructions.
Stragglers' route.
Points/Routes deciphered by the 'B' Service.
U-boat position.
U-boat proceeding.
U-boat tanker.
Contact signals of U-boat.
Contact signals of German aircraft.
U-boat signal picked up by D/F.
U-boat reported by Allied aircraft.
Allied air reconnaissance.
Allied U-boat situation.
Patrol line.
Proposed line.

Actual convoy course with indication of
convoy and Escort Group.

Convoy with close air support.

Course instructions with reference points
and altered course instructions.

Stragglers' route.

Points/Routes deciphered
by the 'B' Service.

U-boat position.

U-boat proceeding.

U-boat tanker.

Contact signals of U-boat.

Contact signals of German aircraft.

U-boat signal picked up by D/F.

U-boat reported by Allied aircraft.

Allied air reconnaissance.

Allied U-boat situation.

Patrol line.

Proposed line.

222

COURSE INSTRUCTIONS AND ORDERS FOR EVASIVE
ACTION FOR A NORTH ATLANTIC CONVOY

Example: SC. 122 8-23 March 1943

- JP — 1st Course instructions of 28 February and 6 March with reference points and stragglers' route.
- 1st order for evasive action.
- 2nd order for evasive action.
- 3rd order for evasive action.
- Actual course.
- Air cover.
- U-boat warning area.
- CHOP-Line.

CINCLANT
COMINCH
Washington
COMNAV
New York
Ottawa
Halifax
CHOP-Line
NSFC

MIELEN-OZHA

Iceland
Reykjavik
Torshavn

AZORES

223